# GREEN LEAVES OF BARLEY:

*Nature's Miracle Rejuvenator*
*An Updated Edition*

## by Dr. Mary Ruth Swope

*WITH DAVID A. DARBRO, M.D.*

**SWOPE ENTERPRISES**
P.O. BOX 1290, LONE STAR , TX 75668
*PHONE: 1-800-447-9772*

***Green Leaves of Barley: Nature's Miracle Rejuvenator***
An Updated Edition

Copyright © 1987, 1990, 1992, 1993, 1994, 1996, 1998 by Dr. Mary Ruth Swope
Swope Enterprises
**P.O. Box 1290, Lone Star, TX 75668**

ISBN 0-914903-41-1

Library of Congress Cataloging in Publication Data

Cover photo: Fields of Halifax, Nova Scotia
Photographer: Larry Beaton,
Typography by Plus Communications, St. Louis, MO.
Printed in the United States of America

Published and distributed by
Swope Enterprises
**P.O. Box 1290, Lone Star, TX 75668**
**1-800-447-9772 or (903)-562-1504**
**Fax: (903)-562-1609**

# Green Leaves of Barley
## Nature's Miracle Rejuvenator

by Dr. Mary Ruth Swope
with David A. Darbro, M.D.
Susan C. Darbro, B.S., English, B.S., Nursing

## Other books by Dr. Mary Ruth Swope:

*Lifelong Health*
*Listening Prayer*
*Spiritual Roots of Barley*
*Bless Your Children Everyday*
*Surviving the 20th Century Diet*
*Some Gold Nuggets in Nutrition*
*The Roots and Fruits of Fasting*

# Acknowledgments

It is with great pleasure that I am privileged to share the medical knowledge and experience of my son-in-law, David A. Darbro, M.D., in this third edition of *Green Leaves of Barley*. He speaks from 32 years of experience in medicine — working to restore the health and well-being of people through his clinical practice and his seminar teachings.

The librarians of three educational institutions deserve special mention for their extreme helpfulness in locating reference materials — Florida Institute of Technology in Melbourne, Florida; Eastern Illinois University in Charleston, Illinois; and the Indiana University Medical School in Indianapolis, Indiana. Special mention goes to Librarians, Dr. Robert and Carrie Chen of Charleston, Illinois.

Deep appreciation is due my secretaries, Gloria Armstrong, JoAnne Mick and Charlotte Bates, who cheerfully made "jillions" of corrections, additions, and revisions. My only daughter, Susan Darbro, accepted with grace the formidable task of writing two chapters — knowing that her days would be totally occupied with my adorable grandchild in his "terrible two's." I am deeply grateful for her excellent contribution.

Miriam Champness brought writing and editorial skills as a true co-laborer in the last days of writing — offering just the right contributions and encouragement to bring this book to fruition. Dale Stone offered invaluable suggestions for improving professional and grammatical accuracy of the final manuscript. Final proofing and editing were done by my step grand-daughter Elise Darbro.

For the hundreds of individuals who answered my green barley questionnaire or wrote me unsolicited testimonials which they consented to be included in Part 2 of this book, I am deeply grateful.

To my one-in-a-million late husband, Don, and my son, Stephen Cornwell, special thanks.

Last, but certainly not least, for strength, health, life, and my years of education, all needed for a task of this magnitude, I give thanks to God.

# Contents

# Foreword

It is my opinion that, if one wants to have vibrant health and be "disease free," one must become a person who studies and applies the scientifically-proven principles of nutrition. There is absolutely no other way to achieve a constant state of wellness without this. All living, rejuvenating, healing processes are intimately related to the work of nutrients.

The whole world has served as a proving ground for this concept. What humans (or animals for that matter) regularly consume in terms of their food and drink can be used as a remarkably accurate predictor of their length and quality of life, their reproductibility, their size, vitality, disease patterns, mental problems, productivity, and so forth.

America is no exception to this. Our diet for the past fifty years has provided convincing evidence, if not conclusive proof, that by accepting a poorer quality diet than our ancestors, we have lowered our standards of health.

After practicing traditional family medicine for fifteen years, I began to study nutrition. To my amazement, I found a plethora of medical literature showing that nutrients could be used as medicines to correct imbalances at the molecular level, which could then lead to reversal of chronic degenerative disease. Up to that time of professional enlightenment, I had used prescription drugs as my primary therapeutic tool.

I am gratified to see improvement in patients with disorders such as chronic fatigue syndrome, candida or Epstein Barr trouble, or patients with circulatory or digestive problems, when using nutrients as the first line of defense. I have come to consider myself only as a servant to the patient's own "physician within." We must encourage or work with the built-in principles and laws that the body uses to heal itself. One doctor is quoted as saying "If we eat wrongly, no doctor can cure us — if we eat rightly, no doctor is needed."

The use of nutrition in medicine is a very old concept. Hippocrates, the "father of medicine" lived from 460-377 B.C. He is credited as saying, "Food is your best medicine and the best foods are the best medicines." I believe the true greatness of Hippocrates, however, lies in the fact that he recognized the necessity of treating illness consistent with nature. He believed that the natural forces within us are truly the healers of disease.

I believe you will find the information in this book both fascinating and helpful. If you are presently experiencing symptoms of less-than-perfect health, I recommend orthomolecular medicine (nutrition) as the first plan of attack to improve your health. In fact, I agree with Dr. Swope that the dried juice of tender, young barley leaves is truly a food with real power. One or two teaspoons daily is an inexpensive, easy way to improve the quality of your present diet. Cells made strong through good nutrition will go a long way in giving you an immune system that will resist the illnesses so prevalent in our society.

*David A. Darbro, M.D*

# Introduction

King Solomon of Bible times wrote, "Of the making of books there is no end" (Ecclesiastes 12:12 KJV). If that was true in his day, imagine the magnification of that truth today when thousands of new books are published monthly in our country alone.

So, why is this book being written? Because, for the first time, millions of Americans are waking up to the fact that they are in less than excellent health. They are realizing that they are without much understanding of how it all happened. They realize too, that they have too little knowledge of how to correct their acquired poor health.

Many people are disenchanted with the medical profession's persistent use of pharmaceuticals without the possibility of a choice of treatment modalities. We hope to offer light (without "heat") that will benefit multitudes of people.

This book will attempt an answer to the two subjects: (1) what happened to my health? — and — (2) what can I do about it? — with special emphasis on the green leaves of barley as an **ideal food concentrate** for helping to correct the problem.

You will find a vast array of subjects, related to powdered barley leaves, thoroughly covered in an easy-to-read manner from reliable sources of information, including recent research studies.

Dr. Darbro discusses the effectiveness of treatment modalities he has found to work successfully with his patients. This is followed by a chapter on my impressions of how the modern diet has impacted the health of Americans. Both of us write from a deep conviction that preventive health measures need more emphasis than they are now getting. We believe that, if you follow our advice, you can really "feel the difference" in your health.

## CHAPTER 1

# Resolved:
# The Physician 'Within'
# Knows Best

*By David A. Darbro, M.D.*

In case you are unaware of what's happening in the field of medicine today, let me put it simply — there's a war going on. Like most wars, its opposing forces are fiercely patriotic to their causes, each side believing itself to be just and right. Like most wars, it is a gravely serious conflict — a fight to the death.

In this war, one side is overwhelmingly larger, stronger, better armed and in a more strategic position than its foe. It is determined to totally annihilate the opposition, to wipe the rebels from the face of the earth. No prisoners are taken in this conflict, no mercy is shown.

You might be wondering why I write this. You should understand, I'm in the thick of a skirmish myself. I'm dodging bullets as I write — in fact, I've already sustained injuries and have the scars to prove it. And as much as I would love to have the security of knowing mine to be the winning side, I must confess I belong to the rebel forces. Although we're small, weary, weak and bloodied, we keep on fighting the good fight. And why? Because of you, dear readers. If we lose our war, you stand to lose your lives.

Although the battle rages in all fifty of these United States, and in other countries as well, the reason you can't see it happening is because it is being fought in the realm of ideas. The contestants: orthodox medicine versus alternative medicine. The place: the minds of people in the health fields. The spoils of war: You.

## HOW I EARNED MY HALO

You are no doubt wondering how a mild mannered doctor from the Midwest got himself involved in this war, and why he is taking time from his busy life to speak to you about it and what all this has to do with the green leaves of barley.

Let me explain.

When I was in medical school, I was like most other students there. I was young and idealistic. I looked up to my teachers, respected what they said, studied hard and never really questioned what lay behind it all. It never occurred to me that we were wrong in our whole perception of health and disease.

Looking back now, it seems obvious that a system of education which takes place in the setting of a hospital, where people are at death's door, cannot teach much about health. Health is, after all, what we're aiming for.

Nor is it any surprise that those of us in the medical profession cannot help regarding individuals who come to us for treatment as case histories rather than people. My warm, personable, humorous, intelligent, skilled acquaintance, Jane Doe, is instantly dissolved into "middle-aged female gallbladder" when she steps through my office door.

As one author sums it up, "By separating the disease from the patient and casting the doctor opposite the disease in a military posture, medicine's logic fixes the doctor's attention on the disease, not on the patient."[1]

And once we identify the disease, all we had to do was plug in the right therapeutic tool, a prescription for the right drug. It all seemed quite obvious: disease was the enemy. My job was simply to fight disease and become a knight in shining armor in the process.

My colleague, Dr. Robert Atkins, describes very well what I want to get across to you about the effect of medical school upon its students. Looking back, I can see I was suffering from what I like to call the Ben Casey syndrome:

> *"Orthodox medicine has entrenched itself within a formalized structure that is surprisingly codified. Centered around the teaching hospital, this structure includes ritual, pomp and ceremony, a hierarchy, a belief system, and a profound faith in those beliefs. It is very like a religion ...*

_"I do not know how many doctors have adopted medicine as their religion, but I suppose they do so in large numbers. Medicine has such an appeal._

_"But as a religion, it promotes a blind emotional attachment to its tenants and consequently, a blind antipathy to what it perceives as heresy ..._

_"Most doctors indulge in medicine-worship to the extent that they cannot be reasoned with..."_[2]

## HOW MY HALO BEGAN TO TARNISH

After I graduated from medical school, I spent fifteen years doing just what they had taught me: to prescribe drugs, saying "I'll see you in two weeks." Gradually, I began to realize my patients never actually got well. If they had high blood pressure, for instance, I could control it by giving them appropriate medication, but the problem itself would return the minute the medication was discontinued.

One day, it dawned on me that all I had accomplished in spending five years and thousands of dollars in medical schools was that I had learned how to maintain disease at an acceptable level. This was a shock. It put quite a dent in my suit of shining armor. (In fact, my armor finally became so beat up I had to throw it away!)

In order to explain my change of allegiance from the medical establishment from which I had come (traditional or orthodox medicine) to the rebel camp (alternative or preventive medicine which I now practice), we need to stop and look at medicine a little closer. We need to examine its historical and philosophical roots, and delve a little into what really makes it tick. Before doing that, however, I must state clearly an important concept.

## HATS OFF TO THE OPPOSITION

Having declared myself one of the opposition, I must make something clear — I am NOT in any way castigating the noble men and women who dedicate their lives to saving the lives of others. The hospitals in this country are first-rate, equipped with state-of-the-art equipment and staffed with skilled technicians, nurses and physicians.

In a medical emergency, there is nowhere on earth I'd rather be. It is necessary to act dramatically in crisis situations, and the medical profession is to be applauded for its skill in dealing with catastrophic illness. My hat is off to the established medical order within the context of crisis care. We have the best in the world, and if you are ill enough to be hospitalized, you need to be grateful to the system as well. The problem is not how the medical system operates in its own context but how it fails to maintain health.

## HOW IT ALL BEGAN

Even the ordinary man on the street can probably tell you the name of the  Father of Medicine — Hippocrates. Four-hundred years before Christ, Hippocrates doctored in his native Greece with such skill that men from all over the ancient world came to learn from him. Even today, young doctors graduating from medical school traditionally take the Hippocratic oath. It is with Hippocrates that the debate which continues to rage today began, and the issue is on which belief system the doctor opts for — to practice from experience or to practice from theory.

The issue might not seem important at first, but when we study it a little more, I hope its significance will become clear. These two methods are known as empiricism and rationalism.

## EMPIRICISM

Webster defines empiric as "pertaining to, founded upon, or derived from, experience: one who relies on practical experience to guide his actions." The earliest medicine was practiced from an empirical standpoint — you might call it the common sense method. I see something that works, so I do it. I might not understand why it works, but the fact that it does work is more important to me than the explanation why.

In the game of medicine, Hippocrates is credited for getting the empiricist ball rolling. He observed that the body has a tendency to heal itself, and called this power the "physis." Later you will see the irony in the fact that we get our word "physician" from Hippocrates' "physis."  He put it like this: "It is nature that finds the way ... though untaught and uninstructed, it does what is proper ... to preserve a perfect equilibrium ... to re-establish order and harmony."[3]

Please pay special attention to the last phrase, because reestablishing order and harmony in the body is what the rebel cause in medicine is all about. Hippocrates taught that nature is the best healer, that physicians should work with nature. He saw the importance in being in harmony with nature.

His teachings concentrated more upon seeing the patient as a unique individual interacting to his own environment than as a patient exhibiting specific disease. Symptoms were regarded by the early empirical physicians as the result of the body's reactions to what it encounters from the outside world, and the goal of the physician was to bring the body back into balance. The emphasis was on the general state of a patient's wellness, not the particular manifestation of a specific disease.

In other words, since he believed the body was capable of healing itself, Hippocrates' task was to promote the general wellness of the body so that it would be strong enough to rid itself of a particular disease. In this tradition of medicine, the overall state of health is addressed, and the goal becomes the strengthening of our adaptive powers.

The doctor is seen as a teacher, an assistant to the physis, not the crucial figure in the healing process. Hippocrates' cardinal rule of thumb was "First, do no harm." Again, remember this, because in the context of modern medicine it becomes significant. The keys to keeping in your mind what empiricism means as it concerns medicine are "practical experience" and "promoting wellness."

## RATIONALISM

Ancient Greece also produced another viewpoint, from which has arisen the medical giants of today. Its most famous proponent was the physician, Galen, who lived several hundred years after Hippocrates, but Galen got his philosophy of medicine from the great philosopher, Aristotle.

Aristotle is credited with being the first person to divide up and categorize knowledge in a thorough, systematic order. The system he used in classifying different kinds of plants, for instance, is still in use today.

All of this, I'm sure we can agree, is very good in and of itself. I have nothing against order, reason and logic, but eventually this way of thought came into conflict with the healing arts previously mentioned. Herein lies the root of the difficulties. What evolved from this overall system of viewing our universe is a constant striving for greater precision in analyzing the world around us. This, in turn, when applied to the field of medicine caused it to rigidly oppose itself to anything it couldn't understand by logic or deduction — Hippocrates' physis, for instance.

## A BRIEF HISTORY OF MEDICINE

Here in the United States, both traditions — empirical and rationalist — were thriving nicely in the beginning. It didn't take long, however for the battle of ideas to follow medicine across the Atlantic, sowing seeds of professional discord. Before long, by the early nineteenth century, the two traditions were locked in combat.

The empiricists practiced a form of medicine called homeopathy, which was developed in Germany by Samuel Hahnemann (1755-1843). The homeopathic way of treating a sick person is to give the individual minute doses of the substance which, if given in large quantities, would cause the disease symptoms to occur. In fact, the dosages that Hahnemann worked with were so diluted that the molecules of the substance couldn't be measured at all.

We do not, even today, understand the mechanism behind the success of this treatment, but it is an undeniable fact it worked (and still does). It didn't conform to the logic of their rational traditions of medicine, but it got results and it still does!

While we're on the subject, please allow me to interrupt our history lesson for a moment. Let's zero in on an important concept. Hahnemann was using the same substance that caused the disease to cure the disease. This is a use of "similars."

Perhaps the easiest way to sum up the essential difference in the two approaches to medicine is to understand that empiricists use "similars" and rationalists use "opposites." The health practitioner who uses similars wants to gently stimulate the patient's healing responses, or physis — he doesn't want to upset the "balance" any more than it is already upset.

A person coming from the rationalist tradition, however, views disease in a completely different manner. He doesn't think in terms of promoting health but rather in terms of fighting disease. What is the enemy? Disease, of course. What needs to be done? Fight and conquer the enemy.

How do you do that? Oppose the problem. Make the body do the opposite of what it is doing. ("Allo" means opposite, therefore, current medicine founded upon the rationalistic tradition is called "allopathic.") The perspective is different here, and leads to wide extremes in selection of treatment.

For example, let's take a person with a diarrhea problem. This patient comes in the office and says "Doc, I've got the runs. What should I do?"

If his doctor is from the allopathic school (which 99.9 percent of doctors in America are), he will very likely prescribe a drug that slows up the movement of the bowel. Since diarrhea is caused by too much bowel activity, he will treat it with the opposite — a substance to slow its normal activity down to almost nothing.

If, however, his doctor is from the empirical approach, he might suggest a very gentle enema to cleanse out the bowel — an action similar to how the body is already coping with this particular imbalance.

So back to our history lesson. By the early 1900's hospitals were a relatively new thing — only to be found in a few urban areas in our country. The men trained in European medical schools and their students naturally gravitated toward these new institutions. They were educated men. Their methods, due to their underlying philosophy of medicine, were strong and interventive. Such things as blood letting, emetics (medicines to make you vomit), cathartics (strong laxatives), and strong medicines containing poisonous mercury were their favorite therapies.

According to Dr. Benjamin Rush, famous professor of medicine at the University of Pennsylvania in colonial times, "The physician must be bold and dictate ... the use of powerful and painful remedies in violent disease ...."[4]

The empiricist practitioners, however, tended to have less formal medical training and were much more conservative in their methods of treatment — milder doses of medications, herbals and botanicals. They served a significant percentage of the population, but were less "high profile," as we would say today.

## ALAS, MR. PRESIDENT

Let's stop here and have you take a test. Following is a description of the last illness of our first President, George Washington, in 1799. I'd like to see if you can guess which kind of doctor he had.

> *"Think of a man being, within the brief space of a little more than twelve hours, deprived of 80 or 90 ounces of blood — afterwards swallowing two moderate American doses of calomel, which were accompanied by an injection; then five grains of calomel and five or six grains of emetic tartar; vapors of water and vinegar frequently inhaled; blisters applied to his extremities; poultice of bran and vinegar applied to his throat, upon which a blister had already been fixed. Is it surprising that when thus treated, the afflicted General, after various ineffectual struggles for utterance, at length articulated a desire that he might be allowed to die without interruption!"*[5]

## BIRTH OF A SACRED COW

The history of medical practice in our country took a very sad turn in 1849, the year the American Medical Association was founded.

Why was it founded? Because the homeopathic physicians, whom the mainstream rationalists openly identified as the "enemy," were having such success in their endeavors to heal. Many more of our forefathers were choosing to go with the empiricists. Naturally, this meant less money in the allopath's pockets, and that was the clarion call to unite and fight. You can imagine what happened.

*"Thus, the AMA began its glorious tradition, spanning nearly 140 years, of unbroken commitment to the same noble ideals — economic self interest and the squelching of all intellectual opposition. Not only did the newly formed APIA bar homeopathic doctors from its ranks, it prohibited its own membership from using any homeopathic techniques. It even barred physicians who referred patients to homeopaths or who worked at hospitals where homeopaths were allowed to practice. With these strong measures, the AMA won the day, and within 60 years there was a near-total uniformity to American medicine, with hardly a dissenting voice to be heard."[6]*

## THE PLOT THICKENS

With the coming of the Civil War, another major change in the face of medicine took place — the rise of the pharmaceutical industry.

Prior to this time, doctors themselves were familiar with the ingredients they prescribed for their patients. Now the compounding of medicines became centralized, doctors no longer needed to bother learning their own business — pharmaceutic companies not only identified their products but also indicated to the physician which disease was to be "cured" by which particular product. Within a very few years, there were literally thousands of patented medicines. "So what?" you may ask. One author explains it quite well.

*"The industry began producing literature to educate the practicing doctor to new diseases and methods of cure using the compounded formulas they had patented. They developed the idea of the industry sending out 'detail men,' sales persons trained to educate doctors, give free samples and provide literature. This strategy is still in widespread use today, but in the 1880's it was of an even greater impact. In many parts of the country, because of poor or nonexistent roads, physicians simply did not travel. There were few conventions and no refresher courses in those days. For many the drug salesman became the key method of "staying up" with medical research. Some of the pharmaceutical houses even sup-*

*plied pharmacists with the financing, pamphlets, and supplies to
begin their businesses. With the drug industry supporting both
pharmacists and physicians, it had no competition except with
itself, and medicine gradually evolved into a drug-industry-orient-
ed treatment philosophy. The tail (Physician approved drug suppli-
ers) was now wagging the dog (the medical profession). Now traditional medicine was ready for seduction." [7]*

## BIG BUSINESS GETS BIGGER

If you can understand the implications of what you just read, what
comes next will be no surprise.

*"The pharmaceutical companies realized how much orthodox
physicians depended on their medical journals, so they began buying them.*

*For example, Parke-Davis, between 1877 and 1883, bought
several successful medical journals, each headed by orthodox
physicians, professors at prestigious medical schools. The cream of
orthodoxy was now being salaried by the pharmaceutical industry.*

*The drug industry's companion technique was advertising. Of
the 250 medical journals in existence in 1906, all but one were sup-
ported by advertising from the drug industry.*

*All this, and more, goes on today. The pharmaceutical indus-
try's efforts to seduce physicians through detail persons, free semi-
nars, drug-testing research, journal ownership, and advertising
should be well known to you all ... Physicians had once been open
to any therapeutic system that appealed to a rationalist's intellect.
Now they assumed that the only answer was pharmaceutical." [8]*

I am the first to admit that pharmaceuticals have saved thousands
of lives and certainly have a valid place in the practice of medicine.

In fact, I've prescribed a ton of them myself. But when we look
at drugs in the larger context of the healing arts, we come up with
some major problems.

## POTIONS OR POISONS?

Even the pharmaceutical industry itself recognizes the obvious:
For each desired action of a drug, there are usually numerous unde-
sired actions — side effects. Every year doctors get a new copy of a
huge book called the *Physicians' Desk Reference*, which catalogues
all the drugs on the market, giving information on their chemical-
structure, how they work, when they should be used, when they

should not be used, how they affect pregnancies, what the correct dosages are and what the warnings and adverse reactions are, based upon testing with real people.

I came across an old yellowing edition on a little-used bookshelf the other day (of course I keep a current issue) — the 27th edition published in 1973 — and randomly opened it. The first thing that met my eyes was "Warning: SERIOUS AND OCCASIONALLY FATAL HYPERSENSITIVITY (ANAPHYLACTOID) Reactions Have Been Reported" and the list was 14 items long.[9] Interestingly, some of these, it states, could be controlled with the use of yet another drug.

Before I am accused of being unreasonable, let me say again that I credit use of some pharmaceuticals with saving thousands of lives that would otherwise have been lost. I am not opposed to using prescription drugs when the need arises, but my point here is that they are dangerous substances, and should be used later rather than sooner.

## RISK-BENEFIT FACTORS

Because the toxicity of drugs is so well known, one of the major tasks of a physician's work is to assess what we call the "risk-benefit factor." In other words, we need to figure out if we harm the patient more by giving the drug or by withholding it. Most weapons against disease are also weapons against health. Sadly, there is much truth to the statement, "We cured the disease, but lost the patient." This is a sad commentary on a profession dedicated to the saving of human life.

## BACK TO THE BATTLEFIELD

All this leads us right back where we started, to the war that's going on right now in your town and mine. Most doctors want to practice medicine as it has been taught to them that is, "... as the science of taking the business of healing out of nature's hands."[10]

They wish only health for the body. But they couple their noble intentions with a resolution (which their medical theory demands) that says, "I will achieve the body's health by imposing my will upon it."[11]

They believe they are right, and they are ready to fight to defend their position — especially those of them who have had no exposure to the empirical side of medicine other than the vehement lectures against the subject by professors they respected and admired.

## WHY BE A REBEL?

You may remember the point at which I noticed the first big dent in my medical suit of armor. I realized I was maintaining acceptable disease rather than promoting health. It's essential to grasp that distinction. Anti-disease is NOT the same thing as pro-health.

When I began to open my eyes to the possibility of there being more medical truth out there than I possessed (this is very hard for a card-carrying AMA type, like I was, to do!), I quickly grasped the significance of this. My goodness! Had I been doing it wrong for fifteen years?

The more I studied, the more I began to see that my methods had to change. I had to do much less of fighting disease and do much more of promoting wellness — so my patients, true to Hippocrates' wisdom, can heal themselves.

Perhaps I should clarify myself here. Obviously, if a person is in an accident and breaks bones or needs lacerations sutured, alternative medicine is not appropriate. Thank God for our fine emergency rooms!

Likewise, if an appendix has ruptured it needs to be taken out by a skillful surgeon in a hospital setting. God bless our fine surgeons! If Mr. Jones is having a heart attack, he needs to have an ambulance take him to the emergency room. In its place, medicine as we know it is good and is needed.

What makes me a rebel in the eyes of establishment medicine is not that I don't appreciate it for what it is, but that I don't see it as the whole answer for the problem of illness in our nation today.

Modern medicine is responsible for eradicating a host of diseases in which micro-organisms are the primary cause. Things like polio, smallpox, tuberculosis and cholera for example, are rarely if ever seen. Yet we still have disease. If medicine has done such a good job of stamping out disease, why are health care costs in the billions of dollars every year? And why are physicians ignoring the use of nutrition as a treatment modality when it is a well-known fact that "...70 percent of all deaths in the United States are caused by diseases linked to the consumption of our diet?"[12]

## WILL THE REAL PROBLEM PLEASE STAND UP

Medicine has done a wonderful job of stamping out a certain kind of disease — the acute kind. But what kills us these days are chronic degenerative diseases. What does that mean? It means that the biggest killers — heart disease, for example — develop gradually over a period of years.

The problem isn't that a patient is at the wrong place at the wrong time and catches a "fatal bug." The problem is that an unhealthy lifestyle and an unhealthy environment slowly but steadily erode the general state of wellness, which causes the body to slowly deteriorate until one day the danger signals can no longer be ignored.

It might seem like the patient suddenly dropped dead of a heretofore nonexistent heart problem but that's not what really happened. The patient had a high fat, high sugar diet for years, and it was slowly but surely clogging up his arteries. He smoked cigarettes, which caused the vessels to become even smaller.

He was under stress for 20 years with a job he didn't like, causing his body to work much harder than it should have. His primary form of exercise was leaving his easy chair to go raid the refrigerator during commercial breaks on TV. He suddenly dropped dead, even though he'd just been to his doctor and checked out fine!

Chronic degenerative disease needs to be reversed — not by drugs and surgeries, but by the changing of lifestyles and environments — by promoting what is healthy. What does this best — traditional doctoring or alternative medicine?

## WHAT IS MEDICINE?

Much of what I've learned since my "awakening" has to do with using nutrition as medicine. This is what makes the average M.D. hot under the collar. He isn't opposed to good nutrition, it's just that he doesn't see it as having anything to do with the practice of medicine. The idea of helping the body in a general way rather than combating a specific problem in the body is totally foreign to him. Furthermore, his training taught him that "scientific proof" is necessary to validate everything. If it's not in his medical literature, it's not any good.

So clinical nutrition, herbal remedies, drugless medicine, and the like, are worthless to him because there's no "proof" they work — no proof that is, in his sense of the word. He cares nothing for the fact that the patients get better — getting better isn't scientific enough. It defies his logic. Here's how one writer explains it:

*"Classical science assigns little value to knowing simply that something works. It assigns a much higher value to knowing how something works. As a result, it's scientifically possible, perhaps even required, to call a therapy 'unscientific' or 'unproven' simply because scientists do not know how it works, even if there's evidence that it does work, and even though knowing how something works doesn't change its therapeutic value."*[13]

## AND AGAIN:

*"I had hay fever, and food allergies so severe that they almost killed me. Cortisone helped, but I didn't like the side effects. Then I tried a natural healing remedy, and both the hay fever and the food*

*allergies went away, without side effects. I'm pleased to be healed and I believe the natural healing remedy did it, or at least helped my body to do it.*

*The very gentleness that pleases patients and tends to avoid side effects also produces a certain conceptual and practical fuzziness that makes proving that the natural healing did it almost impossible, at least to the satisfaction of classically trained scientists. As a result, those scientists generally call natural healing 'unproven' and 'unscientific,' while it is actually neither. It is simply another way of thinking, as logical and internally consistent as medicine, and with its own message of proof."[14]*

## THE DOUBLE-BLIND BIND

Modern medicines demand for proof is the cornerstone of its structure. It doesn't want opinions, it wants proof. What does this mean? When the profession was younger and less sophisticated than it is today, it was satisfied with repeated observations — tabulating and comparing results. However, as the profession grew, so did its demand for precision.

Following the tabulation studies came the demand for placebos (phony medications used strictly to fool the patient into thinking he was getting a drug when in fact he was not). Why placebos? Because the rationalists suspected what the empiricists knew all along — what a patient believes about his treatment affects how the treatment will work. If they could fool the patient, they felt they had real proof!

Today, things are even more complicated. Medical science demands tests in which neither the doctor nor the patient be aware of who is getting the real thing and who is not.

Because many alternative therapies require patient awareness and lifestyle changes, they cannot be proven in a double blind study by definition! It is a perfect Catch 22. As one famous physician astutely put it, "It is easier to cure a hundred incurables than it is to prove that the treatment works."[15]

## THE ROOT OF ALL EVILS

So as not to appear bitter or prejudiced, let me borrow another physician's explanation of what's really going on here:

*"How we all hate quackery! Fighting evil is a noble ideal, and nothing could sound more noble than a war against quackery. What could be a loftier goal than to purge the profession of charlatans, those fraudulent pretenders to medical knowledge who bilk unsus-*

*pecting patients of their life savings, all the while costing them their health and denying them a chance for effective treatment? Certainly, I can think of none — except perhaps to purge the profession of those who use the campaign against quackery to persecute super-competent, innovative physicians whose very success threatens the livelihood of the mediocre.*

*The war against quackery is a carefully orchestrated, heavily endowed campaign sponsored by extremists holding positions of power in the orthodox hierarchy. They work through organizations with names such as National Council Against Health Fraud, American Council on Science and Health and the Quackery Action Council .... The salient fact is this: This multi-million-dollar campaign against quackery was never meant to root out incompetent doctors. It was, and is, designed specifically to destroy alternative medicines."[16]*

Perhaps the most tragic example of this can be found on how cancer is studied — and ignored — by orthodox medicine in this country.

*"The question of research grants is more clear-cut. Here the drug industry itself is often the benefactor, 'paying specifically to have research done on exactly the pharmaceuticals it intends to promote'....*

*"All of this means, in spite of a rather impressive list of clinical studies published in Europe, an anticancer protocol of antioxidant vitamins, including vitamins C, E, beta carotene, and selenium, along with, perhaps, some enzymes and other biologicals, does not get studied at all, while chemotherapy combinations are studied by the thousands under the government's aegis.*

*"It also means, thanks to the stonewalling role of the media (another corporate establishment constituent), that you or your doctor don't even know that such orthodox studies are being conducted, and reported upon. Research on promising biologic approaches should obviously be done, but through the passive resistance technique known as calculated ignorance, no one in authority admits to being aware that there is work that bears replicating. To give a specific example, l find it hard to believe that the officials of the National Cancer Institute, whose entire careers are devoted to knowing about cancer research, would be unaware of conferences in Switzerland and Germany where high quality*

*research papers about successful non-toxic, biologic treatments
are being presented. It is much more plausible to presume that they
are aware of what's going on and choose to pretend that it does not
exist. If you need to know the reason, it's this: The entire concept
of a biologic, non-toxic cancer therapy would signal the beginning
of the end of the highly profitable chemotherapy industry, an
industry that is deeply entrenched in establishment economics.
Acknowledging the biologic conferences would be an extreme anti-
establishment act."* [17]

## HOW I GOT DRAFTED

When I graduated from medical school, or even during the first
dozen years of my practice, had I read this chapter somewhere, I
undoubtedly would have been not only skeptical, but also much
offended. I was a member of the AMA myself, a typical product of
the system. It wasn't until I found myself in King David's position,
cowering under the shadow of Goliath, that I realized many of these
not-so-pretty truths. How did I get there?

Like many other alternative-minded physicians, I totally ignored
"quackery" until I came up against a situation in which all the good
orthodox rules and regulations failed to help a member of my own
family. Desperate, I decided to try an alternative therapy that is, after
first trying it on myself to make sure (as Hippocrates would have
approved) that it would do no harm.

When I had experienced its safety, I tried it on my loved one. To
my amazement, it worked! The patient improved dramatically. I
decided to try it on someone else, and guess what! There was remarkable improvement. This pattern, the hallmark of empirical medicine,
continued. Soon, I had firmly incorporated the "quack" therapy into
my practice — I had turned into a full-fledged rebel!

## THE HEART OF THE MATTER

What was this strange unorthodox therapy I had adopted?
Burning chicken feathers? Taking snake oil? Chanting mumbo-
jumbo over the inert bodies of my poor victims?

No — cleaning out their arteries by means of a drug administered
intravenously in the office. It's called "Chelation Therapy." and it's a
very controversial thing to do. The purpose of it is to clean out
gummed-up arteries and thereby improve heart disease and peripher-
al vascular disease, among other things.

Why is it controversial? Because even though it's been administered thousands of times to thousands of patients with nothing but

good results, according to the AMA it's unproven, and we all know what that means: quackery!

## HOW I LOST MY HALO ALTOGETHER

If my patients had not begun improving, things might have been much easier for me. But, 'unfortunately,' they did get better. So much better that they didn't need to spend $30,000-50,000 on their next by-pass surgery. I suspect that's what did it — cardiac surgeons are beginning to figure out that alternative medicine isn't good for business.

Yes, I lost my halo. I've been threatened with losing my license to practice medicine for doing this therapy. In fact, it's been threatened four different times. Like I said, I really am dodging bullets even as I write.

## BRINGING THE WAR HOME TO YOU

Suppose you think treating cancer with the "cut/ burn/ poison" (surgery/radiation/chemotherapy) method isn't quite what you'd want for yourself or your loved one? What if something you've read in this chapter makes you want to try alternative medicine instead? What if you actually made a firm decision to do so?

A colleague of mine puts it rather well:

*"Now you have just stripped yourself of most of your support system. You will be on your previous doctor's 'bad' list, and so you'll wonder what will happen to you if, God forbid, there is an emergency. You'll be afraid of hospitals, knowing they will surely take you off the new diet and nutrition program you're beginning to depend on. Your insurance carrier will, more often than not, give you various types of 'hard times' in getting your reimbursement. Your friends and some of your family will try to talk you out of your folly and bring you back into the fold, where all the normal people are. You're even likely to hear, or read, that your new alternativist doctor is a quack. And the greatest affront of all is that your new doctor is going to expect you to do your own getting well, he isn't even going to do it for you.*

*"What it all comes down to is that you've lost your security blanket."*[18]

## WHY YOU SHOULD JOIN UP ANYWAY

If underdogs appeal to you, I urge you to join up now — we need your help! If you could care less about the war, I urge you to join up anyway. Why? So you can get healthy yourself and stay that way!

One way to start is to read the rest of this book and get some good nutrition. Take it from a "quack" — green barley juice is really great stuff!

*Note: To support alternative medicine efforts, send your gifts (large or small) to:*

*The American Preventive Medical Association*
*459 Walker Road*
*Great Falls, VA 22066*
*1 (800) 230-2762*

## WHY YOU SHOULD JOIN US NOW?

## CHAPTER II

# Wake up, America ... You're Sick!

As you can see from Chapter 1, medical doctors are required to choose between two major opposing philosophies of medical practice — traditional or preventive medicine. Every other decision they will ever make, with or about patients, is determined by their choice in this matter.

At the same time, all of us also have a choice to make when we shop for medical care. Are we going to accept the "mostly drugstore" or the "mostly drugless" variety of treatment? I strongly suggest we shop at the "nutrient pharmacy" for as near 100 percent of our cell/tissue/organ needs as is possible — accepting drugs only in case of acute illness. In other words, **make "wellness" instead of "controlled illness" your lifetime goal.** Now let's examine a few facts about where we are in terms of our journey toward wellness.

In a recent seminar on orthomolecular medicine (the use of nutrition in the treatment of illnesses) my eyes were opened to the truth about the health of Americans in a new way. A medical doctor was lecturing to other M.D.s and health professionals about the conditions of patients coming to his clinic for treatment. Most of the doctors who lectured and those who listened were preventive health-minded — quite a different breed from the average M.D., who knows little and cares less about nutrition. Frankly, I was shocked by what I heard.

In the first hour of the lecture, only one logical conclusion could be drawn: Americans are epidemically sick and need to wake up and wise up to the reasons for their unhealthiness. Included here are a few of the facts pinpointed for later in-depth consideration at the conference. Hopefully, every reader will have the same response I had to the statistics — to be more attentive to preventive health measures, especially those related to foods and nutrition. Now for the facts.

## DEGENERATIVE DISEASES: A MODERN EPIDEMIC

According to the *Statistical Abstracts of the United States, 1994,* **nearly one million Americans die annually from heart disease.** On the surface this might not appear so shocking, unless we know how these figures compare with those at the turn of this century. There were very few deaths from heart disease then. In fact, the first article to appear in the *Journal of the American Medical Association* on this subject was in 1911. Why, in about 85 years, have we gone from just a few people dying annually from heart disease, to nearly one million? The answer is not simple, but it definitely involves changes in our eating habits.

Statistics from the same source tell a similar story for a whole host of other conditions classified as degenerative diseases. For instance, **deaths from cancer have also been climbing steadily** since the turn of this century. In 1995 more than half a million people died from cancer. That figure is up 225 percent since 1960! Why? The American Institute of Cancer Research estimated in 1984 that as many as 60 percent of these cases could be related to diet!

**Diabetes Mellitus is another very prevalent ailment** among Americans. While it has been identified as a sickness since the time of the Greeks, it is only since the turn of this century that it has become rampant. About 10 million Americans now have active cases, with nearly 600,000 new cases reported annually. Again, this illness is related to our diet.

Before leaving this subject, it is encouraging to note that two physicians studying diabetes for a lifetime have made very similar public statements about this disease. They said, in essence, that if patients were to lower their weight to normal and keep it there, adult-onset diabetes would disappear in slightly more than 80 percent of the cases. Losing extra pounds will also lower high blood pressure in the majority of cases and improve stamina and resistance to many other diseases.

Americans are spending around $210 billion annually on heart disease, $14 billion on cancer, $10 billion on diabetes and, now, $8billion in Medicare alone on osteoporosis (porous bones). This is a condition once only identified with grandmothers. These elderly women, far past menopause, often suffered broken hips because the hip socket became so spongy it wouldn't hold the body's weight. Their hips break and then they fall, in 80 percent or more of the cases.

Be that as it may, the **United States now holds the record for osteoporosis**. Approximately 30 percent of women past menopause have it, and, for the first time in our history, it is also being found in young women and in men. These facts are unheard of in many countries. Why? What is happening in America that isn't happening in other countries?

## WAKE UP AND WISE UP

Of course, I do not have a complete answer based on longitudinal research, but I have strong suspicions. There are many research studies which allude to the fact that high phosphorus and/or phosphoric acid (found in meat and soft drinks) pulls calcium out of the bony structures (bones, teeth, and nails) in the process of digestion and assimilation. This has a disastrous effect on bone density, leaving them porous and spongy.

Dr. Yoshihide Hagiwara, in his book entitled *Green Barley Essence*, put it this way:

> *"The combination of soft water and phosphates wreaks a terrible effect on the bones ... when the amount of phosphoric acid was increased beyond a certain limit (in a study to show the effects of foods on the bones of mice), bone malformation occurred in the mice. Further increase of phosphoric acid in the food of pregnant mice yielded 40 malformed fetuses out of 100.*
>
> *Nor am I alone in this conclusion. A government warning was once issued to a manufacturer of a certain world-famous refreshing drink for its suspected effect on the bones of children, because of the large amount of phosphoric acid contained in it."*[1]

According to the National Soft Drink Association, in 1993 soft drink consumption has increased to the point that Americans are consuming 51.8 gallons per person per year. That compares to 10.4 in 1950. At the same time, consumption of meat, poultry, and fish hit an all-time high in 1993. According to USDA figures, per capita consumption reached 221.7 pounds a figure 19 percent above the previous 75-year average of 186 pounds.[2] I believe these two changes in the American diet are largely responsible for our extremely high incidence of osteoporosis.

## *DEGENERATIVE DISEASES: REALLY BIG BUSINESS!*

**The incidence of kidney stones in the U.S. has doubled in the past 20 years.** The cause, in 75 percent of these cases, is thought to be related to our high sucrose (white sugar) consumption. Two to five hours after heavy sugar intake, there is a burst of two times the amount of calcium released into the urine. Another cause is our high acid-ash diet due to high meat intake. When calcium is pulled from the bones, it is released through the kidneys, resulting in stone formation before it is excreted.

This scenario could go on and on, but I will end it here by listing a few more of the degenerative diseases that are epidemic in our country, with a word or two about each.

**GALLSTONES** — About 1,000 Americans are operated on daily for this condition. In Africa, according to Dr. Dennis Burkett, there have been two cases in the past 20 years!

**DENTAL CAVITIES** — Almost every American has them; we consider deteriorating teeth "normal." In many parts of the world you couldn't find a single case to show a dentist.

**PROSTATE GLAND PROBLEMS** — About 70 percent of American men over 60 years of age have this problem. We hold the international record in this category!

**ULCERATIVE COLITIS** — Two million of us have it. It is unknown in many parts of the world.

**GASTROINTESTINAL PROBLEMS** — Billions of dollars are spent on over-the-counter products and prescribed drugs for our belching, bloating, flatulence, and constipation.

**VERICOSE VEINS AND HEMORRHOIDS** — These problems are now epidemic among us. More fiber and exercise would help prevent and/or alleviate these cases.

**HYPERTENSION** — Thirty million Americans have it and are being medicated with drugs costing billions of dollars. Just 30 years ago it was an uncommon problem.

**GOUT AND ARTHRITIS** — Millions in our society are now receiving medication to alleviate suffering from these two conditions. Traditionally diseases of the elderly, these conditions now encompass all age groups, including young children. Recent figures show one in seven to have some form of arthritis, costing us $13 billion annually in medical care and lost wages.[3]

**DIVERTICULITIS** — This is another disease with strong dietary implications and it is epidemic in the United States. However, in countries where fiber has not been removed from food supplies, it is practically unheard of.

**IATROGENIC DISEASES (M.D. INDUCED)** — These are some of the saddest cases to me. All drugs have side-effects, and there is no known antidote for effecting a cure in many cases. Millions are ill because of this.

**HYPERACTIVITY** — This condition affects millions in our society and is a condition which has not come of age yet! No cases were known as little as 20 years ago!

**ALLERGIES** — These are big business for our medical doctors. Millions are ill from these hard-to-diagnose and harder still to cure allergies to foods, drugs, and chemicals.

**ATHEROSCLEROSIS AND ARTERIOSCLEROSIS** — These conditions are household words today. Millions of Americans have faulty circulation and hardening of the arteries.

**CIRRHOSIS OF THE LIVER** — This is as much an epidemic in America as one of its major causes — heavy drinking of alcoholic beverages. About 6 percent of our population is now classified as "escape drinkers." Teenage alcoholism is greatly increasing. Some physicians today say the rising rate of liver damage among even the very young can be traced to the appalling consumption of soft drinks. It is safe to say that the need to maintain the health of one's liver ranks at the top of the list.

**MENTAL ILLNESS** — This condition is also increasing among us. About half of our diseases are thought to originate from our minds and negative emotions — anxiety, fear, hate, jealousy, bitterness, unforgiveness, grief, and the like.

A list of diseases affecting Americans in epidemic proportions would not be complete without mentioning hypoglycemia and candida albicans. Physicians differ in opinion on these disorders. In fact, some still doubt the significance and/or prevalence of either condition. Most who treat them, however, would acknowledge that our high intake of sugar and refined carbohydrates is one of the basic offenders in both disorders.

## LENGTH AND QUALITY OF LIFE CHALLENGED

Is it an exaggeration to say that the majority of Americans are either directly or indirectly involved with family or friends who are chronically and/or terminally ill? Life at its best is being challenged and at more than the personal and family level. The collective health of our citizens is beginning to adversely affect all aspects of our national life — especially our economic and social vitality.

The diseases we suffer now do not come upon us overnight. It takes years for the body to break down and permit disease to overtake us. Cancer can take as long as 20 years to develop. Heart disease can be 30 to 40 years in the making. Arthritis, kidney stones, osteoporosis, diabetes, hardening of the arteries, and many, many others fall into this category.

During the interim years, many people are not sick enough to be symptomatic. We have at first what is called "vertical disease." A person with vertical disease is still able to stand up and walk around, but he doesn't feel good. The symptoms are tiredness, depression, muscle pains, insomnia, lassitude, lack of motivation, and many other diffuse symptoms such as constipation, indigestion, gas, and headaches.

"Horizontal disease," the symptoms that cause you to stop work and lie down in the sick bed, come later. But, come it does! Millions can attest to the surety of this fact, as we have just heard from the doctors themselves.

## CAN MODERN MEDICINE BE 'HAZARDOUS TO HEALTH'?

We are told that more than 100 million Americans are suffering from these "new degenerative diseases" of this century to one degree or another. Why should this be true?

We have more physicians of all types, more hospitals and clinics of various kinds, more highly specialized nursing services, more health spas, and more health-education programs and the like than any country in the world. So, isn't it amazing **when compared to other nations, we are not near the top now in terms of overall health?** "Why?" you ask.

The answer is not simple. Keep in mind that Americans DO live in the highly stressful fast lane on a seven-day-a-week basis. This is accompanied by a high intake of drugs (prescribed, over-the-counter, and on-the-street types), and by much smoking, alcohol abuse, and high levels of junk food intake. The modern-day air, water, and soil pollution create tremendous assaults on our health, as do the negative lifestyle factors that cause the breakdown of DNA, RNA, and our immune systems. Certainly, all of these play a part in our unwellness.

## HEALTHFUL REMEDIES 'HIDDEN' IN OUR PAST

A great weapon to conserve or restore health that we have permitted to be almost buried is the use of natural remedies for fighting disease. Such things as charcoal, herbs, teas, hydrotherapy, heat and cold, fasting, massage, exercise, nutrients, foods, rest, and pure water are almost unheard of as treatment modalities. **Sadly for us, the** standard medical procedure in America now includes only four approved treatment methods: **prescription drugs, radiation, chemotherapy and surgery.** Tons of legitimate research is done worldwide, as well as clinical observation and testimony, to show that these four treatment modalities **should be used mostly for "crisis" medical treatment** or as a last resort. They have very little effect in stopping the course of, much less preventing, our modern-day diseases.

In books like Dr. Robert Mendolsohn's *Confessions of a Medical Heretic and Medical Mayhem,* it is obvious all is not in "unity" in the medical profession. Plenty of highly trained physicians believe the drugs presently being used are poisonous and useless, if not lethal, to sick people. It is a well-documented fact that prescription drugs, even antibiotics, can be hazardous to your health. Allow me to share a case in point.

## WHY AM I TAKING THIS?

A 26-year-old friend of mine was diagnosed as being "hyper" and "nervous." Her physician prescribed the following drugs for these problems — Navane, Symmetrel, and Amitriptilyne. These drugs had no meaning to me until I looked up their possible side effects in a well-known book. I list them here with the hope that you will become a wiser patient — one who asks more questions of your physician before you swallow his prescribed medication.

**NAVANE SIDE EFFECTS** — Rapid heartbeat, lightheadedness, low blood pressure, drowsiness, restlessness, insomnia, rash, itching, hives, exaggerated sunburn, dry mouth, blurred vision, nasal congestion, constipation, increased sweating, increased salivation, changes in appetite, nausea, vomiting, weakness, fatigue. Long-term use may lead to involuntary movements of the tongue, jaw, mouth, or face.

**SYMMETREL SIDE EFFECTS** — Most frequent are: fear, faintness, depression, congestive heart failure, psychosis, urinary retention, hallucinations, confusion, irritability, loss of appetite, constipation, nausea, lightheadedness, fluid retention. Less frequent: dry mouth, headache, vomiting, insomnia, weakness, skin rash, visual disturbances.

**AMITRIPTILYNE SIDE EFFECTS** — Change in blood pressure, skipped or pounding heartbeat, heart attacks, congestive heart failure, stroke, hallucinations, delusions, anxiety, agitation, insomnia, manic behavior, tingling sensations, tremors, seizure, ringing in ears, dryness of mouth, blurred vision, constipation, urinary retention, skin rash, fluid retention, depression, low bone marrow count, blood disorders, nausea, vomiting, diarrhea, cramps, enlargement of breasts, and more and more. *[NOTE: A more complete chart on the side effects of drugs has been included in the Appendices.]*

Does this stimulate you to learn about the possible side effects of the drugs YOU are taking? I hope so. Maybe it will also encourage you to seek alternate treatment modalities for your symptoms. Nutrition would be a first place for you to look. At least one thing is certain — **proper nutrition has not one possibility of an iatrogenic (doctor induced) consequence.** Foods in their natural state do not have damaging or life-threatening side effects. The side effect of totally natural foods, for example — *fabulous health!*

*[Author's note: I find five prescriptions to be a very common number being taken by older citizens today. Remember this: There are nine major categories of drugs being used now and only one of them treats a cause; all others treat symptoms.]*

The overuse of surgery has also been exposed again recently on TV. The uselessness of surgery for cancer has been known for at least three decades. Your surgeon, of course, will be the last to admit it. As long as he can find people to submit to his scalpel, he will! But, it is well known in medical circles that surgery causes cancer cells to spread.

Doctors at Kaiser Hospital in California have shown radiation to cause new cancers to form where the X-rays of the first radiation burn normal tissue. We've all heard of the experiences of relatives, friends, and acquaintances who have suffered the extreme nausea, weakness, hair loss, and general debilitation resulting from this radical treatment method. Or, maybe you have experienced it yourself.

Chemotherapy, too, is not as effective as we have been taught to believe. Studies have clearly shown this treatment has limited success in prolonging life for patients who undergo it. While it destroys cancer cells in the blood, it also damages healthy cells and generally weakens the immune system. In addition, chemotherapy causes cancer cells to grow stronger to fight the drug "offender."[4]

If Americans want to get well from cancer, heart disease, arthritis, diabetes, obesity, and a whole host of debilitating conditions, in my opinion, they will have to find nonorthodox treatment modalities involving nutrition and other remedies "provided by nature" as the major components.

From the way doctors treat us these days, it is easy to get the wrong impression — and millions apparently have. It is easy to think we have heart disease because we don't have enough Digitalis or

Lanoxin in our blood. Or, we have high blood pressure because we lack Aldomet or Aldactizide. Maybe my acid indigestion is because mother didn't know to give me Maalox or Tagamet! These are the "answers" we are given to our symptoms when the cause of our condition is TOTALLY IGNORED. The cause, more often than not, is too little or too much of a natural nutrient — an amino acid, a vitamin, a mineral, fiber, water, a carbohydrate, an enzyme, or a fat.

The general public, to a growing extent, is now beginning to connect disease with dietary deficiencies or overindulgences. It is so obvious, even to the untrained population. The amazing thing is that the medical profession continues to ignore this association and neglects to seek answers where they can so easily be found — in foods and nutrition.

The predicament we find ourselves in is not new. Jesus told about a woman sick for 12 years with a hemorrhage. She had suffered from doctors, had become poor from paying them, and was no better, but, in fact, worse. (Matt. 9: 20-22)

## MODERN MEDICINE DENIES TREATMENT CHOICE

Will the AMA ever offer the necessary expertise in nutrition by its professionally trained doctors? I don't know. Benjamin Rush, M.D., and signer of the Declaration of Independence, foresaw years ago what has happened to us when he wrote, "Unless we put medical freedom into the Constitution, the time will come when medicine will organize into an undercover dictatorship ... the Constitution of this Republic should make special provision for medical ... as well as religious freedom."

Yes, it is true. We are being successfully denied freedom of choice in treatment modalities for our diseases. Doctors who disagree with standard medical procedure are being put in prison and denied the right to practice medicine if they ignore the rules of the "undercover dictatorship."

Perhaps this will change when the grass roots public refuses to accept the presently accepted standard medical procedures and opts for self-treatment, if necessary. Or, they have the option of attending clinics outside of the continental United States, such as those in Mexico or Bermuda. In any event, it seems apparent that there is a principle at work in the medical profession that has been time tested in many other fields of endeavor. **Monopoly always encourages poorer service at higher prices.** Millions of Americans are seeing this phenomenon for themselves in medicine today. We desperately need preventive health modalities of treatment not yet available through orthodox medicine.

Before you get the idea that I am against doctors, let me clarify one point. It is not doctors that I am against — it is the abuse of power by doctors. It disturbs me that a professional organization should have the power to keep practitioners from learning and practicing those treatment modalities they think work best, especially in regard to the preventive and curative powers of good nutrition.

But let me say this, on behalf of the many competent and ethical medical doctors who serve us wholeheartedly. I firmly believe them to be part of God's plan for curing sickness and relieving pain. What I am saying, about degenerative disease in particular, is that each one of us must take our own part in prevention much more seriously. Is it "merely a coincidence" that **the conditions that have NO medical cure are the ones each of us can and must take personal responsibility for preventing?** The tragedy of degenerative disease is that the conditions which are so often fatal by the time they require attention from a doctor are the very same conditions that are almost entirely preventable through a personal commitment to good nutrition.

## CHANGES IN DIET: THE REAL ENEMY OF HEALTH

As a nutrition educator with 56 years of experience in foods and nutrition, I have a strong bias to offer as one of the major true causes of our poor health. We have almost buried our strongest and best weapon to fight disease, general malaise, and poor health — a fresh, healthy food supply grown on an organically fertilized soil without the aid of sophisticated chemicals by the hundreds, if not thousands! Our high-tech foods cannot be nutritionally compared to the foods we were growing and consuming in this nation at the turn of the century.

Let me illustrate in Table 1 why I believe scientists, who report that our soil is not producing crops as full of nutrients as in former years, are correct. These are government figures.

## TABLE 1

### COMPARATIVE NUTRITIVE VALUES
### OF ONE CUP OF BROWN RICE (1950 & 1993)*

| ONE CUP | 1950 | 1993 | % LOSS |
|---|---|---|---|
| Weight (gm.) | 208.0 | 195.0 | 6 |
| Energy (calories) | 748.0 | 230.0 | 69 |
| Protein (gm.) | 15.6 | 5.0 | 68 |
| Calcium (mg.) | 81.0 | 23.0 | 72 |
| Iron (mg.) | 4.2 | 1.0 | 76 |
| Vit. $B_1$ (gm.) | .66 | .18 | 73 |
| Niacin (gm.) | 9.6 | 2.7 | 72 |

\* Composition of Foods — Raw, Processed, Prepared, Agriculture Handbook No. 8, United States Department of Agriculture, 1950 and 1993.

**Today, a large part of our foods can rightfully be called food-less** (produced totally in our big labs), drugged, embalmed, dead, coal-tarred, artificial, skeletonized, polished, processed, refined, sterilized, oiled, sprayed, waxed, degenerated, unclean, frozen, canned, dried, impure junk, and now the threat of IRRADIATED FOOD. (Is it logical to believe humans can tolerate food treated with atomic waste?! My answer is no!)

All of the above foods can be put down the esophagus with varying degrees of ease and pleasure, but they do not feed the cells with the nutrients required to create and sustain healthful bodies. Those come only from a "natural" food supply. Spray-dried green leaves of barley are an excellent example when they are organically grown without chemical fertilizers or pesticides and are not refined or processed with high heat or freezing.

The effect of refining foods is well illustrated in Table 2. See for yourself why preventive-health-minded professionals urge us to eat whole-grain "natural" cereals in preference to those that have been highly altered by processing.

## TABLE 2

### NUTRITIVE VALUES OF VARIOUS TYPES OF RICE*

| One Cup | Whole-grain brown | White | Minute Rice |
|---|---|---|---|
| Calories | 720.0 | 708.0 | 355.0 |
| Carbohydrate (gm.) | 15.0 | 13.1 | 7.1 |
| Protein (gm.) | 154.8 | 156.8 | 78.4 |
| Calcium (mg.) | 64.0 | 47.0 | 5.0 |
| Iron (mg.) | 3.2 | 5.7** | 2.8** |
| Vit. B1 (gm.) | .68 | .86** | .42** |
| Vit. B2 (gm.) | .10 | .06 | 0.0 |
| Niacin (gm.) | 9.4 | 6.8 | 3.3 |

* Composition of Foods — Raw, Processed, Prepared, Agriculture Handbook No. 8, United States Department of Agriculture, 1950 and 1993.
**Has been enriched with artificial chemicals

It is easy to see that, although the calories are twice as many, the protein and complex carbohydrates are twice as rich, calcium is 1100 percent more, iron and vitamin B are more, and niacin is 300 percent greater. Whole grains are natural, and anything natural is of better quality than that same food refined or processed. **It has been estimated that in America today 65 percent of our foods are processed and 60 percent of us are epidemically sick!** Is this one reason why?

It is relatively easy to find statistics on the changes made in recent years in our eating and drinking habits. Let's consider our beverage consumption first. It is in this arena that our most startling changes in food consumption have taken place since the 1950's. We are drinking more alcohol, beer, and soft drinks, but less water. Few Americans realize, however, what these changes mean in terms of health. I want to give you my opinion of the one change, in addition to alcohol beverages, that has the most potential for tragedy in terms of health. That is our consumption of soft drinks as the replacement for water to satisfy "anytime" and "all-the-time" thirst.

Cola drinks are consumed daily in larger amounts than water without a thought as to their chemical content. Recently, a television viewer wrote to tell me that a male friend of hers, a college student, was drinking 3 quarts of cola daily. That is equivalent to eight 12-oz. cokes containing 72 teaspoons of sugar (1-1/2 cups!!) In addition to the sugar, there are from 240 to 464 mg. of caffeine, depending upon whose figures you believe!

Research has shown that **24 teaspoons of sugar eaten in one day reduces the number of bacteria that our white blood cells will destroy by 92 percent.** I can't begin to guess what eating 300 percent more sugar (just in drinks not counting desserts, cereals, candy, alcohol, etc.) would do to this young man's immune system. Of one thing I am sure. Research studies have convinced me that he can expect bone deterioration (including loose teeth in his jawbone), kidney stones, diabetes, heart disease, cancer, tooth decay, back problems and a host of other illnesses.

In regard to the man's caffeine intake, a government booklet on the subject says we get a pharmacological or drug effect on a 60 to 100 mg. dose of caffeine. It continues to be reported that **caffeine is associated with high levels of cholesterol which cause heart disease, and with low levels of the "good kind" of cholesterol that protects the heart from disease. Caffeine also encourages acquisition and natural development of peptic ulcers, diabetes, and hypoglycemia.**

There is research evidence to show that caffeine causes an alteration in the chromosomes in the nuclei of cells and may be linked to cancer. I wonder what effect a daily intake of 300 to 400 percent MORE than a drug-effect dose would have on the body. I feel sure it is devastating to health, especially the heart and nervous system.

The young man's friend who wrote wanted me to contact this brilliant prelaw student and warn him about the dangers of soft drinks in this amount. Should I, or is that meddling? I am not sure, but I am willing to share my opinions with readers and hope that you will warn your family and friends. I will talk more about the damaging effects of sugar in another context.

Other facts about changes in our beverage consumption patterns are important to know. Whereas in 1950 our thirsts were quenched predominantly by milk, water, and coffee, they are now satisfied by soft drinks, fruit drinks and "six packs" (beer).

In the amounts being consumed, the fruit drinks add too much sugar. In a sense, they too are addictive. Both soft drinks and beer contain addictive substances, and addiction leads to overconsumption. Overconsumption leads to obesity, one of the important at risk factors for cancer, diabetes, heart disease, and a host of other degenerative diseases.

The addictive element in beer is, of course, alcohol. "Alcohol is itself a drug, sedative, tranquilizer, hypnotic, or anesthetic, depending on the quantity consumed."[5] Unfortunately, alcoholic beverages do not have their fair share of nutrients — certainly not enough to justify their high caloric content.

With the exception of beer, commonly consumed alcoholic beverages are devoid of nutrients. Beer has a small amount of thiamine, nicotinic acid, and protein; otherwise, all its calories are from alcohol. To make things even worse, regular drinking is known to affect food choices; irregular meals and ingestion of foods poor in nutrient density are the common patterns. This is often aggravated by gastritis, diminishing the beer drinker's appetite for normal foods.

At this point in time, 70 percent of our young adults drink beer regularly, while 12 percent are classified as "heavy drinkers," whose pattern is daily consumption. The bright side of this is the simplicity of improving the nutrition of this portion of our population. If you have been having trouble with your stomach and you are a regular beer drinker, try leaving out the beer. It may be both the simplest and the cheapest cure you've ever had!

Soft-drink consumption is up almost 500 percent since 1950. While TV ads have lulled us into believing soft drinks are a "fun food" for those who are "smart enough" to live the "fun type" lifestyle in the fast lane, I predict the time will come when we would give anything if we had not listened. As with heart disease, cancer, and diabetes, it takes years for the body to break down and permit disease to develop. So, it will take years for soft-drink users to get symptomatic, but, if they live, they are headed for horizontal disease! **The "Pepsi Generation" hasn't a ghost of a chance of escaping the kind of health problems that will remove them from the fun life in the fast lane!**

## FOUR CASES AND A QUESTION

Let me illustrate my statement with four recent case histories. The first was told by a surgeon friend. A 3-year-old child fell from his tricycle and broke his elbow. When my friend operated to repair the damage, he discovered the child's bones were too spongy to tolerate a metal pin or a wire wrap. He had no alternative but to put the arm on a board and send him home for nature to take its course in healing.

Why were a 3-year-old's bones so degenerated? The surgeon surmised it was because the child's mother and grandmothers for two or three generations were **heavy meat, sugar and soft-drink** consumers. These foods pull calcium out of bones. It is easy to see the accumulative effect — finally there isn't enough calcium in a woman's body to produce a baby with healthy bone tissue. This surgeon believes he is seeing many young people today (athletes especially) with poor quality bones.

The second case is one I witnessed personally. A wife and mother of three (ages 9, 7, and 2 years) told me her story. The bones in her feet were soft and deteriorating. Her doctor advised her not to stand on her feet more than 1-1/2 to 2 hours per day. She complained to me that it was not possible for her to get housework done in that length of time. She was worried how she was going to manage. When I asked what the doctor thought caused her problem, she said, "I'm a Dr. Pepper freak. I have one on the hour every hour that I'm awake."

When I related this story to another doctor friend of mine, he said, "Did you tell her that if she continues her soft-drink habit, it won't be too long until her hip sockets will disintegrate and she will not be able to sit in her wheelchair? And, following that, she could conceivably be confined to a hospital bed for the rest of her life." I forgot to tell you she is only 37 years old!

The third story pertains to society in general. At a 1986 annual meeting of a state dental association, a keynote speaker said **an estimated 10 million Americans have loose teeth.** The bottom line was that there is presently no method of successfully tightening teeth in deteriorated jawbones.

The speaker did not deal with possible causes. The tragedy to him was that perfectly good teeth were having to be pulled as a precautionary measure. There was the potential danger of patients losing teeth in their sleep and possibly choking to death on them. I kept wanting him to warn against continued consumption of soft drinks and red meats and sugars. I wonder if he has enough nutrition knowledge to understand what is happening!

The fourth case comes from a 1995 seminar experience. A nurse asked, "Can you explain why there is a rash of babies being born now without skulls?"

Yes, I believe I can — too much meat, too much sugar and too many soft drinks in our diet. Let me summarize my reasons for **not consuming** soft drinks and wanting you to do likewise.

## DISEASE FLOURISHES IN AN ACID pH
## COLA-TYPE DRINKS ARE ACID

All kinds of soft drinks are very acidic, especially colas. In order to neutralize a glass of cola, it takes 32 glasses of high pH alkaline water.[6]

**CERTAIN SOFT DRINKS AND CANCER MAY BE RELATED**

Fransisco Contrares, M.D., said, "Cancer is like a plant cell; it can't live in an oxygen-rich environment." Cola drinks make our bodies poor in oxygen. [7]

## SOFT DRINKS OFFEND THE KIDNEYS

A study of over 1,000 men with a history of kidney stones showed, "There was a clear-cut difference in the group's experiences, with much less renal colic in those who had avoided soft drinks." [8]

## COLA DRINKS PROVIDE ZERO NUTRIENTS, LIKE HARD LIQUOR AND SUGAR

Nutritionally, soft drinks are low in value. In soft drinks, every element of nutritional importance, except calories, is **zero**. Soft drinks are like hard liquor in that respect.

## CAFFEINE IS ADDICTIVE; COKES PROVIDE IT

Caffeine is a drug and it acts as a stimulant to the central nervous system. "In the amounts presently being consumed, it can cause insomnia, nervousness, irritability, anxiety and disturbances in the heart rate and rhythm." [9]

## BIRTH DEFECTS ARE A POSSIBILITY

We have known for generations that caffeine is not for pregnant women or children; it is a stimulant with definite drug effects.[10]

## ANOTHER PROBLEM: CARAMEL COLORING

Cola drinks contain caramel coloring, which, according to some researchers, has genetic effects and is a cancer-causing suspect.[11]

## BUBBLES AND FIZZ - NOT INNOCENT; MAY BURN HUMAN INSIDES

The bubbles and fizz in soft drinks can potently burn human insides; this is caused by the phosphoric acid and carbon dioxide.

## SUGAR - SUGAR - SUGAR: A WHITE DECEIVER

Soft drinks use predominately three types of sweeteners — saccharin or aspartame in the diet-type and sugar, cane syrup or corn syrup in the regular drinks. The adverse effects on health by all of these is well-known and easily varified in scientific literature.

## ALLERGIES: WITH OR WITHOUT HIVES CAUSED BY SOFT DRINKS

Dr. George M. Halpern, Division of Allergy of the University of California Davis School of Medicine, says that diet soft drinks may cause allergies. Acute or chronic hives may be the symptoms.

## SOFT DRINKS DISSOLVE YOUR TEETH AND BONES

Pour Coke over an extracted baby tooth or a 10-penny nail and see it totally dissolve in a few days!

## METABOLISM CAN BE ALTERED: THAT SPELLS TROUBLE

Heavy soft drink consumption can interfere with your body's metabolization of iron and diminish nerve-impulse transmission.[12]

## MORE REAL SYMPTOMS

Cola drinks can interact adversely with antacids, possibly causing constipation, calcium loss, hypertension, nausea, vomiting, headaches and kidney damage. Soft drinks can decrease the antibacterial action of penicillin and ampicillin.[13]

### *BLOOD PRESSURE ALTERATION: ON THE HIGH SIDE*

Diet sodas that are low in calories but high in sodium; no wonder high blood is a very common ailment in our society.

Now that you know this information, how will you respond in regard to your eating habits? Allow me to make an observation about my many friends, most of whom are Christians. They love to quote Hosea 4:6 about their favorite soap box concern, "My people perish for a lack of knowledge."

While it IS true we need adequate, sound knowledge before making behavioral decisions, I sometimes think there is another problem at work! In the area of nutrition, for example, I've found people perish almost as often because they refuse to obey known facts. They know, for example, deep-fat-fried foods and foods high in fat content (like most hamburgers) lead to disastrous heart problems. But, where is their favorite Main Street restaurant and what is their daily menu selection there?

They also know sugar is supposed to be bad for them, but how often do they reject sweet food solely on the basis that it has too much sugar in it for good health?

So, I ask you to consider this question. Which is worse, ignorance or disobedience? Each of us must decide and our decision will pack a real punch for good health or degenerative disease — the type epidemic in America today.

Because of space limitations, it is necessary for me to end this scenario. This means many relevant subjects and issues must be ignored and totally neglected. Hopefully you have gotten the major point from the subject matter covered — **Americans are sick and need to change their thinking about the relationship between diet and health as well as diet and disease.**

## THE GOOD NEWS AFTER THE BAD NEWS

After all this bad news, you will be glad to hear that there is some good news. First and foremost is the good news that **you are in charge of what you put into your own body.** You will find in this book (and in my two earlier books, *Nutrition for Christians* and *Are You Sick and Tired of Feeling Sick and Tired?*) plenty of practical suggestions and a whole new way of looking at your eating habits. If you put them into practice, you will find that you can change!

But there is some extra-special good news: I have discovered a food concentrate (one teaspoon is equivalent to two handfuls of barley leaves) that I believe has the nutrient power to get you "over the hump" with a lot less pain and strain — the vacuum-dried fresh juice of young green barley leaves.

I think it is so special because it supplies the very nutritional elements the American diet has become deficient in! It's just as if our wise Creator put it together especially to cleanse and strengthen us as we seek to make the basic changes we need to get our eating and cooking habits in line with the realities of good nutrition. And, you know, I believe He did!

## THERE IS ANY ANSWER TO OUR DILEMMA

As a way of helping you make better nutritional choices, thus changing eating habits to decrease your chances of degenerative disease, I am including some recommendations. You will find them in the Appendices at the back of this book.

The first is a list of the USDA's dietary guidelines proposed for Americans in 1978. These points and the others that I have added to them make an excellent overall nutritional guide.

Next, you will find a list of dietary guidelines aimed at lowering excessive cholesterol in your diet and strengthening your heart and other vital organs — the Cardiovascular Health List. (See Appendix A.)

Finally, you will find, in Appendix E, a chart produced by the American Institute of Cancer Research in 1984. I want to share it with you because in my estimation, it is an accurate summary of the beliefs of many preventive-health-minded doctors and authors like myself. I highly recommend that you study it carefully and begin to incorporate its principles into your "daily three."

In conclusion, one last word of advice. Do not have a cupboard and refrigerator "clean-out night" in which you go through and discard all your "unhealthy" food. That only leads to total chaos and bilious (as well as rebellious) spirits! It doesn't work for the great majority. Instead, **establish the habit of making small improvements daily.** Drink a few less soft drinks daily as you increase your consumption of pure water. Eat a healthful main dish some night for dinner instead of grilled pork chops with boxed au gratin potatoes. Forsake the doughnuts one morning in preference to shredded wheat topped with oat bran and so forth. You will be surprised to see how easily you can improve your food intake by using this technique.

Surely you see that this means changing your shopping habits. Planning menus would, of course, be the ideal way of assuring that you make changes and that you have the foods on hand to do so. If you can't get that organized, do it your way — BUT DO IT, and do it daily. It only takes 21 days of changed behavior to establish a "new" habit.

Of course, I could not end this chapter without sharing again one of my strongest convictions. **The green leaves of barley truly are a food with real power — nature's miracle rejuvenator!**

## CHAPTER III

# Barley:
# The Botanical Aristocrat

Barley, according to historians, is a well-known grain cultivated from the remotest antiquity. It is mentioned 37 times in the Bible. *Unger's Bible Dictionary* says, "A wild species, found in Galilee and northeastward to the Syrian desert may be the original stock from which all cultivated varieties were derived."[1]

Barley is the fourth most important cereal grain behind wheat, rice and corn, according to the *1986 World Book Encyclopedia.* Sorghum, oats, millet, and rye follow.[2] The world produces nearly 8 billion bushels a year.

Barley is available in several forms and is used for different purposes. In the United States, the majority is ground or rolled for use in mixed feeds for animals. Pearled barley is ground in a revolving drum until hull and germ are removed. As you would suspect, much of the nutritive value has been removed in the processing. This, of course, is the form in which Americans consume it most often in cooking. Sometimes barley flour is used in making bread and in baby cereal.[3]

## A PROFILE OF BARLEY
Some practical facts about barley are these:

* It is the first grain to ripen in the spring; wheat is next and takes 4 to 6 weeks longer to mature.
* Because it is hardy and thrives in high altitudes and northern climatic conditions, it is not attacked by bugs, molds, fungi, or worms, which abound later and in warmer climates.

- Barley is 67 percent carbohydrate and 12.8 percent protein —
  a "perfect" ratio of the two as claimed by modern scientists.
- Barley brought rejuvenation and renewal to the health of the
  ancient people whose winter diets were meager. It will do the
  same for us today.
- Regrettably, in America 54 percent is used in animal feed.
  Another large proportion goes into brewing beer and ale.

## A SPIRITUAL DIMENSION

There is another interesting thing about barley. The Bible says
God told Moses to have the Israelites bring a sheaf of the first barley
harvested to their priest. "He is to wave the sheaf before the Lord as
it will be accepted on your behalf; the priest is to wave it on the day
after the Sabbath"(Lev. 23:11,NIV).

As I began researching that passage in the Jewish historical
books, Jewish encyclopedias, and other reference works, the
words came alive. I knew that barley had deep "spiritual" meaning. It was barley that ripened first and was the sheaf used in
ancient times as well as this very day to celebrate what is called
the Festival of First Fruits. This is recorded in Leviticus 23:9-11
(KJV). "... bring the first sheaf of the harvest to the priest on the
day before the Sabbath. He will wave it before the Lord in a ges-
ture of offering." But what did all of that mean, and how was it
related to my life in the 20th century? I kept studying until I
uncovered deep, rich morsels of truth.

My own thoughts and those of friends and biblical scholars have
been published in book form under the title *The Spiritual Roots of
Barley* and is available by writing to Swope Enterprises, Inc. (See
order form in back of book.) You will be inspired even more to use
and share about the green leaves of barley.

But let me leave you with a challenging thought. God required
"perfect" animals for all Jewish sacrifices. I believe God intimated
to Moses that barley leaves are the "perfect" food in the plant
kingdom. Dr. Hagiwara's research confirms that barley leaves are
the "near perfect" food.

## GLEANINGS ABOUT BARLEY FROM OTHERS

I will pass two stories on to you as they were given to me. I
assume no responsibility whatever for the authenticity. I believe they
will be of interest to you.

## A STORY FROM DENMARK

An M.D. who visited a farm family in Denmark one summer told me he had never forgotten the difference between Danish and American barns where cows were milked. Danish barns were absolutely odorless, even when fresh manure was on the straw-covered floor — but not so in American barns. The smell of manure was sometimes quite offensive.

When he asked the farmer about this observation, he was told that the reason was because of the barley in the cow's diet. Barley is a natural deodorizer, he said. Is that the truth? I believe it is. (See Chapter VI on chlorophyll for more information.)

A North Dakota farmer told me the same thing about the barley's deodorizing properties. Both barley grass and grain are filled with many enzymes. In addition, green barley is full of chlorophyll. Both aid in digestion and, when food is perfectly digested, waste from the intestinal tract is "clean" and odorless.

I'll add my humor to this already amusing story, so I can change the subject while you are still laughing. My strong suspicion is that the front end of a barley-fed cow is also sweet and odorless. I'll wager that a "cow kiss" would smell better than the breath of your own beloved Bowser!

## A NORTH DAKOTA FARMER TALKS ABOUT BARLEY

After I began to work on this book, I met a farmer from North Dakota. He later wrote me a letter which I want to share with you. Here are his statements about barley.

*"In this area, barley is known as a healer of the land due to its ability to grow in alkaline soil. Some soils that virtually would not grow anything but kochia weeds or foxtail will, with some cultivation, produce barley quite well.*

*I personally had an area on the farm that, since my childhood remembrance, was unable to grow anything. I had cultivated for one summer and planted it to barley in the following spring. It produced approximately 70 bushels per acre!*

*Also, I once went to a neighbor whom I respect very highly as a farmer. I put a question to him: 'What are some of the most important truths or secrets you have found in your farming life?' His first reply was, 'SEED BARLEY!!!'*

*He continued, 'One of the most mellow and productive pieces of land I know of is Gissell's farm.' I knew barley had been seeded for 12 years in a row on that farm."*

The thing he said that excites me is that barley is considered a healer of the land. If the land is healed, isn't it logical to assume that it will produce healthy food which will build healthy bodies or cause unhealthy bodies to rejuvenate themselves?

Another thing my friend wrote also excites me. He said,

*"Barley straw is favored by cattle as a feed. I have seen pregnant cows in January (our winters here are severe then) walk away from good foliage to eat barley straw. I know several ranchers who make its use central to their feed program.*

*I want to present you with a grain of thought here. Soil experts, when looking at nutrient requirements for a cereal grain, want to know how much nitrogen, phosphorous, and potassium is available. The Agriculture School experts stop here. But some renegades have seen that is fictitious — depending on what pH is in existence in the soil. They call this 'tied up' nutrients if the pH is out of a narrow acceptable range.*

*A move was on 10 years or so ago to add a fourth element to the standard nitrogen, phosphorous, potassium. It would have been either organic sulphur or lime to adjust the pH. In doing this, much of the tied up elements would have released merely by bringing the pH to a preferred range."*

My friend then asks the question,

*"Can this principle be applied to humans and the blood pH? Do all factors start doing their jobs properly by taking green barley (which is highly alkaline, as opposed to our acid-rich diet) to adjust our blood pH?"*

My answer to this is definitely, YES! Read Chapter VII for an understanding of this subject.

This is another illustration of how well integrated God has made everything which was created. The soil pH affects the growth and health of all the plants just as the pH of the body fluids control the digestion and assimilation of foods and the release and use of nutrients in humans and other animals.

The green leaves of embryonic barley plants are the most alkaline of any of the numerous green plants tested. For those who require an antacid after a meal in order to "feel good," a daily intake of a teaspoon or two of a pure green barley powder might very well eliminate the need for "artificial" preparations, which Americans are using at the cost of a half billion dollars annually.

## TWO WHO RECOMMEND BARLEY WATER

Author Joseph Kadans writes that barley is mild and nutritional enough to help those with stomach ulcers and diarrhea. He also believes it helps prevent loss of hair and improves the condition of the nails of both hands and feet.

According to Mr. Kadans, barley water has been beneficial to those with gravel stones and high fever. He feels it may be useful in asthma because of a substance in the grain, hordenine, which relieves bronchial spasms.

To prepare a good barley drink, Mr. Kadans recommends taking 2 oz. of whole-grain barley and boiling it in three parts of water until the quantity of water is reduced by one half. The liquid remaining is considered good for bowel disorders, especially if 2 oz. of sliced figs are added during the cooking.[4]

Nelson Coons writes that some believe barley water is a "first food" for feeding infants who have kidney and bladder disorders. Mixed with lemon, barley water is an excellent drink for those suffering from bronchitis, asthma, and sore throat.[5]

While these ideas do not call for the use of barley juice, I included them here to show that the barley grain is also a valuable food for health. In fact, Hippocrates said, "Concerning nourishment, I think barley gruel is better than all other cereal foods in taking care of acute diseases; the finest barley should be used."[6]

This background on barley is provided to give a perspective on the real contribution barley grain has made through the ages to the health of all living creatures, including man.

## THE ABC'S OF GREEN BARLEY JUICE

The discovery of the amazing restorative power of the powdered juice of green barley leaves was born out of a personal tragedy. A Japanese medical doctor and research pharmacologist, Dr. Yoshihide Hagiwara, lost his health at the age of 38. He first tried to regain it by taking modern drugs and megadoses of synthetic vitamins and minerals, without success.

He then tried ancient chinese herbal remedies and cleansing diets, with only slightly better results. When he sought healing in a diet rich in natural enzymes, raw chlorophyll, natural vitamins and minerals, and polypeptides (amino acids), he found — the "physician within" brought back his health!

I believe that millions of people today can attest to the effectiveness of eating raw, natural, unprocessed, organically grown food in the building, repair and maintenance of healthy, disease-free cells in our bodies. Yes, **when we remember our nutrition, we can usually forget disease!**

Before Dr. Hagiwara selected barley leaves as his choice of "green foods" for product development, he spent ten years studying the roots, stems, twigs, leaves and flowers of more than 300 green plants at all stages of maturity. (Read his book, *Green Barley Essence,* for full details. See order form in back of book.)

Finally, he found the ONE plant that was superior to all others. About it he wrote: "My research has shown that the green leaves of the embryonic barley plant contain the most prolific balanced supply of nutrients that exist on earth in a single source."[7]

After reading his book and studying his data, I am convinced that his powder of green barley leaves is indeed the prince of all green products. He found the right plant, the right growing methods, and developed and patented the right process for extracting and drying the juice.

After personally visiting his extensive research laboratories and his processing plant in Japan, I am convinced that his green barley product will always be unexcelled. I especially like the product he produces which has the addition of small amounts of powdered brown rice and kelp. These foods enhance the natural vitamin and mineral values which are so lacking in our modern diet.

There are now several other companies producing and marketing green barley products —most of which are not more than two to four years old. However, I know of no other product resulting from the extensive and continuous scientific or medical research equivalent to Dr. Hagiwara's work in Japan. If there is another pharmacologically pure green barley product on the market, I have not found it.

In 1988, Dr. Hagiwara was honored by thousands of scientists and businessmen from all over the world, commemorating his 21 years of research and product development. It is little wonder that he has developed a food concentrate with such "power," considering the efforts put into the development of this food.

## REAL, LIVE GREEN BARLEY LEAVES YOU CAN DRINK!

Let me summarize the virtues of the dried barley juice I use as a part of my daily diet:

- The barley is grown organically, without artificial chemical fertilizers.
- No chemical sprays (pesticides, fungicides, herbicides) are used on the plants.

- The processing plant is "on site" so that the barley is harvested and processed with a very short time lapse.
- The special drying process sprays the juice in a vacuum at about 97° F for 2 to 3 seconds without subjecting the nutrients to destructive processing methods. Not even the enzymes are destroyed.
- It is immediately refrigerated until it can be bottled. It is kept as fresh and near "natural" as possible. I think of it, not as a "product" or vitamin preparation, but as fresh, raw juice from young barley leaves — a food with REAL POWER.
- It is a powder similar in texture to instant coffee or tea (except for its emerald green color), and is just as easy to use (although, of course, you destroy the enzymes if you mix it in anything hot.) A teaspoonful (2 gms.) contains approximately 6 calories and is equivalent to 100 gms. (Two big handfuls of young barley leaves). It is also available in caplet form.
- Regarding its taste, the ads say it's like spinach or green tea, but to me it's closer to how the lawn smells after its just been mowed! Your cow would love it, but your spouse may not! But, in V-8 or carrot juice, it's almost imperceptible. In any case, when dissolved in anything cold to drink, it reconstitutes itself to be substantially the same as fresh raw juice.

Because of the preparation method, most heat-sensitive components (proteins, including enzymes, as well as peptides and other components) remain in their natural state right along with heat-stable materials (minerals and polysaccharides). Since the barley is harvested at an early stage, before the nutrients are concentrated in the heads of grain, it is still full of growth material and juvenile factors that are undoubtedly useful to our own cells and tissues.

The chapters that follow will detail the nutritional value of young, raw, "alive" green leaves of the barley plant — the "aristocrat" of plants and the granddaddy of all cereals.

Included here are brief explanations of the protein content and "nutrient boosters" added to the product. All other components of it are covered in detail in subsequent chapters.

### PROTEIN

Young barley leaves are an excellent source of all the essential amino acids. (From these the body can make all of the other amino acids.) By weight, it is more than 40 percent protein which, according to Dr. Hagiwara, is 90 percent usable. To give you a source of comparison, a hamburger is about 20-22 percent protein and it has the added disadvantage of being 40 percent or more of fat, with choles-terol-building properties in addition.

All proteins are not created equal! The body can use proteins in some foods better than those found in others. Proteins from plant sources are very easily digested and assimilated. Not all, however, contain the full range of amino acids required for growth, repair, and maintenance of tissue. Barley juice powder is not among that group — it contains them all.

Many Americans seem to have the wrong idea about protein. In their minds is the idea that we need MEAT to grow "big muscles" with "great strength" and "great endurance" the ability to work long hours at hard jobs and without much fatigue. This is not at all true. Plant proteins are excellent at achieving the above goals as long as they are properly combined and consumed at the same meal. For example, rice and beans make a protein that will achieve the same body functions as meat. Please believe that!

Many studies show vegetarian diets, which incorporate adequate amounts of grains, legumes, nuts, sprouts, etc., produce healthy peo-ple. A biblical story is a good one to illustrate this.

In Chapter 1 of Daniel, he and his three friends refused to eat the king's food. After 3 years of a vegetarian diet with only water to drink, the king said of these four youths: "And in matters requiring information and balanced judgment, the king found these young men's advice 10 times better than that of all the skilled magicians and wise astrologers in his realm" (Daniel 1:20, TLB).

In recent years, a California nine-year study compared Seventh-Day Adventists with the general omnivore population of California. It showed Adventists significantly healthier in every test with less degenerative disease and more productivity in their work, etc. Vegetable proteins are well utilized by the body and have the added advantage of adding no fat or cholesterol to the diet. That is another reason I am excited about powdered green barley.

## NUTRIENT BOOSTERS: POWDERED BROWN RICE AND KELP

Very small amounts of powdered brown rice and kelp have been added to the green barley powder I use (but not to other products by Dr. Hagiwara) for two basic reasons. They contribute to an improve-ment in texture, which results in better shipping qualities as well as improved shelf life. The main advantage, however, is that these two foods fortify some essential elements in the American diet and complete the nutritional balance of the product. There are good reasons for these conclusions.

Sea vegetables, such as kelp, are known as collectors of energy and concentrators of nutrients, "... they contribute significantly to a solar-based world food-and-energy production system."[8]

"Kelp is one of the best sources of iodine; it is also rich in B-complex vitamins, vitamins D, E, and K, calcium and magnesium. It is beneficial in maintaining the health of the mucous membranes and in providing the nutritional support required to prevent such conditions as arthritis, constipation, nervous disorders, rheumatism, colds, and skin irritations."[9]

A third author spoke of kelp as being used by the Japanese to treat goiter (enlargement of the thyroid gland in the neck). He also said anyone taking thyroid medicine should consult with his/her doctor after taking powdered green barley leaves for a few weeks. You might need to take less, or do away with your prescription medicine altogether. It has certain amino acids which act as a gentle stimulant to the mucous membranes and lymphatic system and has long been recognized as a guardian against high blood pressure, especially amongst the elderly. By promoting the balanced absorption and distribution of nutrients in the body, it is also beneficial to overweight and underweight people by helping to restore their normal weight conditions.[10]

My own experience with those regularly taking this product is that many have experienced a normalizing of their weight and also a lowering of blood pressure. Kelp might be one of the contributing ingredients that brings health to the cells and, therefore, relief of symptoms in these two conditions.

Brown rice contains generous amounts of a number of vitamins and minerals. While the measure of brown rice in this food is small, it augments our supply of vitamin A, E, $B_1$, $B_2$, $B_6$, biotin, niacin, pantothenic acid, folic acid, plus the minerals of calcium, copper, iron, magnesium, manganese, phosphorus, potassium, selenium, sodium, and zinc.[11]

Hopefully you can see, by now, that this green leaves of barley product is a food with real power.

## A LAST MINUTE REPORT

On Thursday, April 26th, 1990, United Press International reported in newspapers nationwide a most interesting new discovery about barley. Reporter Karen Klinger reviewed a study by Montana State University.

The study compared people who ate a diet high in barley with those who ate a lot of wheat products. The results showed some of the barley eaters experienced drops in cholesterol of up to 15 percent after four weeks. By contrast, the wheat eaters had either the same or higher cholesterol levels at the end of the study.

It was postulated that the fiber in barley (beta-glucans) was responsible for the lower cholesterol blood levels. Oats and barley contain significant amounts of this fiber, but wheat does not.

Tests done by the same researcher, Rosemary Newman, on laboratory animals indicated that another substance in barley, (an oil called tocotrienol, which is related to vitamin E), also plays a role in reducing cholesterol.

Hopefully this research will serve as a spring board for further study of the nutritional benefits of barley — making it the super aristocrat of the grain family.

## CHAPTER IV

# Cell Health
# Is True Wealth

If it could be expected that all scientists in the world agreed on a single fact, I believe they would agree on this, **"Life begins, is maintained and ends at the cellular level."** The health of single cells holds the key to the health of the whole organism.

Why is this? Because single cells clump together to form tissues and tissues cluster to form organs. Thus, to keep individual cells healthy is to experience health in the whole body. In reverse, when individual cells become unhealthy, tissues can become unhealthy, and if unchecked, disease can result in the death of the whole person.

## A BACKGROUND GLANCE AT CYTOLOGY

Let's begin with a little history. The study of cells (cytology) dates back to 1665 but it was not until 1840 when microtechniques improved, that much was understood about the fluid content of cells — the true substance of life. It was at this time that scientists first concluded that all plants and animals are composed of cells.[1]

Three basic principles about cells have not changed with time. They are:

• Cells are the units that make up all living matter.

• Cells are units that carry on the function of all living things.

• Cells come from pre-existing cells.[2]

A typical cell has two major parts — the nucleus and the cyto-plasm. Cytoplasm refers to all the material inside the cell, except the nucleus. It is composed of carbohydrates, proteins, fats, ions, and small compounds that differ from cell type to cell type. Cytoplasm appears as an unorganized mass — a scene like you might see in a kaleidoscope but that is not at all the case. Research shows nature has done it again! It is marvelously complex but very specifically and perfectly structured for effective functioning.[3]

The nucleus of the cell is often referred to as the cell's "control center." It has the coded information in it for the manufacture of pro-tein within the DNA; and so holds the key to the manufacture of all building blocks and enzymes.

Cells are not merely little sacs of chemicals, enzymes, and fluid. They also contain highly organized structures called organelles, which are essential to their functioning. Without one of the organelles called mitochondria, for instance, more than 95 percent of the cell's energy supply would cease immediately.[4]

**Cells of a similar type that are grouped together are called tis-sues.** Tissues of one kind depend upon other kinds of tissues to sup-ply some of their needs to carry out their specific functions. An exam-ple of this interdependence of tissues can be illustrated by muscles whose primary function is movement.

Muscles cannot move without oxygen supplied by the blood tis-sue. Neither can they move without food from the digestive tract, which in itself is a complex system of various tissues. Muscles also require regulation of movement in both type and amount, which is provided by the tissues of the nervous system. The body furnishes us many illustrations of the interdependence of cells and tissues such as this one.

In addition, there are also organs involved in body functions. **Organs are simply groups of tissues joined together to perform specific tasks** — for example, the stomach. The stomach lining is one kind of tissue, and the stomach muscles that cause the food to be thoroughly mixed are another kind. The gastric glands that secrete the digestive juices are a third kind, and are different from the nerve tis-sues which signal the emptying of the stomach. A full description of this one organ would require several pages.

## THE MAJOR FUNCTIONS OF CELLS

From these facts, you can see that cells are the basic units of life and they are ultimately and uniquely responsible for all the functions of living matter. Their duties are very specific, but when they are considered collectively, all the functions of the organism are perfectly met when the cells are healthy.

This brings us to the subject of what determines the health status of individual cells. The simplest answer to that question that I can come up with is this. **The health of individual cells is determined by the ability of the cells to carry out their full range of functions.** These are:

- The enzymatic breakdown of foods to provide more than 40 known nutrients for the building, repair, and maintenance of tissue, and for energy.
- The absorption of dissolved substances into cells to serve the same functions as listed above.
- Synthesis, or putting together of organic compounds from smaller units obtained from digestion and absorption or some other synthesis reaction in the cell. This results in the functions of cell growth, secretion, and replacement of worn-out cellular parts.
- Cell respiration which results in the release of energy from the final stage of the digestion of food.
- Cell movement and the movement of substances inside the cell which determine its efficiency in functioning.
- Excretion of waste products (toxins and the "clinkers" of metabolism) from cells. Some waste materials to be removed are soluble others are nonsoluble and nondigestible.
- To maintain a steady state within a cell (called homeostasis) which permits its existence and formation of new cells.[5]

The book *Fearfully and Wonderfully Made* by Drs. Paul Brand and Philip Yancey, dramatically describes the narrow range of circumstances which must be present for cells to live and reproduce while they maintain homeostasis (a steady state). Every cell works constantly in this "dynamic equilibrium" state of existence. Once there is too great a change in the set of conditions required for functioning, the cell dies and the organism can lose its equilibrium and also die. Homeostasis cannot be maintained under unfavorable cell conditions. Let's see now what some of those required conditions are and how they work.

### THE REQUIRED ENVIRONMENT
### FOR HEALTHY CELLS

Now, just what is cell environment? As I see it, it is twofold in nature — the internal and external structure in which the cell lives, moves, and has its being. Research on this subject could be endless. My goal is to lay a foundation and readers may add to these ideas for years to come.

## CELL TEMPERATURE

*Internal (Intracellular) Environment.* The cell functions normally within a narrow range of temperature. For most persons under normal conditions, this ideal heat is around 98.6°F. The body temperature may fall to 85°F.-90°F. without creating cell problems; it may endure a temperature of 77°F. without death. But, cell damage will accompany this experience and medical treatment will be required. Temporary circulatory impairment will probably occur, and local tissue damage presents a threat of gangrene following the thawing.[6]

Conversely, cells cannot continue to function when the body temperature rises above 104°-106°F. Cells begin to be damaged or destroyed throughout the whole body, especially in the brain where, unfortunately, they cannot be replaced. Organs are also damaged during periods of extremely high fever, the liver and kidneys especially. This damage can be severe enough to cause death. That is why it is necessary to keep a person's body temperature below 104°F., if possible, during a time of illness.[7]

You can see from this that healthy cells have a temperature range in which they function maximally. A higher or lower temperature creates cell, tissue, organ, and "whole system" problems.[8]

## CELL pH

A second direct internal environment factor to healthy cells is pH — the acid-base balance. Cells function best when the pH is within the rather narrow range of 7.35 to 7.45. Enzymes within the cell are also affected by pH. A highly acid or highly alkaline cell environment will cause an improper functioning or a total cessation of functioning.

## CELL STRESS

A third factor which affects the normal working of a cell is the presence of drugs (chemicals) unnatural to the cell. All prescription drugs are toxic and have multiple, negative side effects; all create cell stress. All create the need for the type of healing that only nature can provide. Let's examine the physical effects of alcohol (since millions of Americans are involved in its consumption) to illustrate this environmental factor. A few of these effects are as follows:

- Causes the cells of the mouth and throat to dehydrate and become numb.
- Irritates and inflames the esophagus cells, the stomach, and the duodenum, the lungs and the liver.

- Often causes ulceration, bleeding, and perforation (making holes in the walls) of the above organs.
- Interferes with normal functioning of the nerves.
- Poisons the cells of the respiratory system and liver.
- Poisons brain cells, causing them to malfunction, atrophy, or die.
- And, much, much more![9]

## PURE WATER AND CELL FUNCTION

The presence or absence of sufficient amounts of pure water within the cell is the last internal environmental factor affecting the health of cells to be discussed here. The principal fluid medium of the cell is water. The fluid nature of water enables both dissolved and suspended substances to move or flow within the cell. It is a well-known fact that **millions of Americans drink inadequate amounts of water for optimal cell functioning.** The action of electrolytes (minerals and charged particles) is hindered, the production and functioning of hormones is adversely affected, the digestion of food is stymied, and many other cell activities are thwarted by the presence of less than an adequate supply of water.

*External (Extracellular) Environment.* One example here will suffice to illustrate this point. Cells are dependent upon the extracellular fluid around them to carry oxygen from the lungs to the tissues and to remove the carbon dioxide.

This fluid is in constant motion and is rapidly mixed by the blood circulation flowing past the cells for maintenance of cellular function. "Therefore, all cells live in essentially the same environment, the extracellular fluid."[10]

A number of pathological conditions obstruct this blood flow and interfere with cell health. Some of these are: removal of lung tissue, blood clots in the lung, traumatized fatty tissue clogging the lungs (as is often the case in breast surgery), emphysema, collapse of a lung, etc. When blood flow is decreased and the oxygen supply to the cell is diminished, the cells cannot receive either nourishment or oxygen and death is the end result. These skimpy illustrations serve to show, then, that cell environment truly does influence cell health.

Cells are perfectly capable of living, growing, reproducing, and performing their special functions only so long as blood, muscles, organs, glands, and body fluids bring them the proper concentrations of oxygen, glucose, vitamins, minerals, amino acids, and fatty substances required by our body's internal environment.

## HEALTHY CELLS REQUIRE HEALTHY FOODS

After fifty years of interest and experience in nutrition, I believe I have an insight into nature's original design for healthy cells that is accurate. My knowledge level is inadequate for explaining the concept fully in scientific terms, but I think I can help you get my point.

If we begin with the biblical account of man's origin (we were made by God from the dust of the earth, Gen. 2:7, KJV), it is easy to explain the rest. In Genesis 1:11 we read, "And God said, Let the earth bring forth grass, the herb yielding seed," and in verse 12 it reads, "And then God saw that it was good." This took place the third day of creation, whatever that means!

On the sixth day of creation, the Bible says that God created man and woman. In Genesis 1:29 it says, "And God said, behold I have given you every herb bearing seed, which is given upon the face of all the earth, and every tree, in which is the fruit of a tree yielding seed; to you it shall be for meat." Webster's dictionary lists as the first definition of meat, "food, especially food, as distinguished from drink."

Now this is the simple, but profound teaching I want to share. It seems to me that God has created a magnificent human body and then every perfect provision for its growth, maintenance and repair of tissue (healing), without any opportunity for a physical or chemical conflict.

One further thought: the discovery by man of the presence and purpose of DNA and RNA only confirms my understanding of the healthy cell concept. There is a recipe in every cell — put there by God to tell it how to reproduce itself, to energize itself, to empty itself of waste and to heal itself when attacked by "foreigners."

If they are given the proper ingredients in the right amounts at the right time, cells will reproduce themselves and live in health without the use of any outside substance. A Nobel Prize was given to the scientist who proved this point by keeping a chicken heart alive in a test-tube for years and years, just by providing it with nature's cell recipe and removing the toxins that were given off by it as it used the nutrients.

You will notice from this verse (Gen. 1:29) that there are three distinct types of vegetation mentioned grass, herbs and trees. It is my belief that someday scientists will prove that these three kinds of vegetation, along with pure air, pure water, enough rest and enough exercise will hold the key to as perfect health as it is possible to have on this planet.

Luckily for Adam and Eve, they were supplied with an abundance of whole, natural, pure, fresh, ready-to-eat, delicious foods —

the exact substances needed for healthy cells. **The supplies of fruits, vegetables, whole grains, legumes, nuts, seeds and berries were more than sufficient to sustain life in perfect chemical balance.**

Yes, truly, God put upon this earth every ingredient needed to promote and sustain cell life. In addition, I believe He also put on this earth the stems, roots, leaves, and bark containing every ingredient necessary to change a sick cell to a healthy cell. Regretfully, this aspect of cell health cannot be further explored here due to space limitations.

Let me crudely illustrate how I believe our cells are feeling about the American diet with its processed, refined, "artificial" and junk food. Let's say that a brain cell corresponds to a biscuit recipe. It requires flour, shortening, salt, baking powder and milk. Given high quality products in the right amounts with the right mixing techniques and baking methods, excellent biscuits (healthy cells) can result every time.

But think of it this way. Instead of shortening, we use axle grease; for flour, we substitute cement mix; we add a little gunpowder to replace the leavening agent; sand replaces the salt; some polluted liquid replaces nature's pure, raw, fresh-from-the-cow milk. What happens to the brain cells? Is it any wonder that we have tumors, cancers, aneurysms, Alzheimer's disease and a host of other conditions related to not having the right ingredients in the brain cell recipe?

Multiply this nutritional travesty three times a day, most days and weeks of the year, and it is easy to see how our poor quality foods are negatively impacting the health of our cells. **Can you not see that cells are perfectly capable of living, growing, reproducing, healing themselves, and performing special functions only so long as the blood, muscles, organs, glands, and body fluids bring them the proper concentrations of vitamins, minerals, amino acids, fatty substances, oxygen and glucose required by our bodies ' internal environment?**

Let's end our lesson on cell food this way: All of the functions of our bodies depend upon the health of our organs; the health of our organs depends upon the health of the tissues that comprise the organs; the health of the tissues depends on healthy individual cells; the health of the cells depends upon the supply of nutrients and oxygen and liquid in the blood; the supply of nutrients in the blood depends upon the foods we eat. Natural foods are the most perfect sources of all the nutrients needed or required for health. **Lifeless cells make lifeless people just as surely as "dead foods" make dead people.**

If you have come with me this far, you probably agree with me about the source of health — our marvelous, self-restoring, self-healing, aggregate of 75 to 83 trillion cells, aided by a sound mind and healthy spirit. Neither medicine nor surgery, nor the absence of germs produces health. It is the proper functioning of every part of the body, with adequate amounts of pure air, pure water, healthy food, exercise, and a strong immune system, to mention a few.

## CELL NUTRITION: HOW TO CHANGE IT
## FOR THE BETTER

The typical American diet definitely needs improvement. You will find recommendations in Appendix A. In addition to what you find there, I make one further recommendation — a teaspoon or two of the powdered juice of green barley leaves daily. It is one of the most nutrient-dense foods you can buy to provide cells with elements crucial to their optimal functioning.

Remember this, too. Another way to improve one's health through diet is to **omit** toxic foods such as soft drinks, tea, coffee, spices, chocolate, foods that contain preservatives, foods that are dyed, waxed, sprayed with chemicals, etc. This in itself is often enough change to trigger a better health response from your sick, malnourished cells. The elimination of white sugar and white flour is also an excellent step to take to improve cell health.

## CELLS ALWAYS SELECT THE BEST

Cells always respond to an improvement in the quality of your diet. An article by Dr. Stanley Bass, D.C., explains this so well it is included in the appendices for you to study. Regardless of the extent or length of time you have had sick cells, they will make a herculean effort to improve when given the right nutrients. Our bodies ARE programmed for HEALTH, not illness. I hope you will begin to try a little harder to cooperate with nature's plan for using sound nutrition principles to achieve robust health.

## HEALTHY CELLS REQUIRE A HEALTHY MIND

A positive mental attitude is absolutely crucial to the concept of healthy cells. There is a constant interplay between our mental and bodily reactions. Hans Selye, M.D., has given us a whole library of books showing the relationship between many common diseases and our inability to adapt to everyday strains and stresses in life's experiences.

As Dr. Selye and others have demonstrated so powerfully, many nervous and emotional disturbances, high blood pressure, arthritis, gastric and duodenal ulcers, cancer and certain types of sexual, allergic, cardiovascular, and kidney malfunctions appear to be essentially "diseases of adaptation."[11] It is through learning to adapt to our constantly changing circumstances that our various internal organs, especially the nervous system and endocrine glands (thymus, hypothalmus, thyroid, pancreas, sex glands, parathyroid, and pituitary) help our cells to experience true homeostasis — a standing steady, regardless of circumstances. In the absence of learning to adapt to these life situations, we succumb to innumerable illnesses and diseases.

In recent research in such areas as the role of loneliness in obesity and the role of laughter and tears in healing, we are reinventing the wheel as we put the mind and body back together in our concepts of health. We used to think depression often resulted in obesity. Now, there are indications that obesity can produce depression; it is all one system. One draws little arrows at one's peril — unless the points are at both ends.

One of the most important theories of drug addiction speaks to a body/mind state called "dysphoria" as the starting point for drug abuse. It's just what it sounds like, the opposite of "euphoria." It refers to a state in which you "feel bad" in body and mind. We have often thought of ill health resulting from mental problems. Now we are beginning to realize mental problems, addictions for instance, can arise from a state of poor health.

Poor health may start with a clogged up metabolism, with its resulting low energy level. Is low energy a "symptom" of depression, drug abuse, etc.? Or is it the cause? Good nutrition has tremendous potential in these areas, because it simply, demonstrably, can change people's energy levels and outlooks for the better. And, dried green barley juice is certainly a food that is rich in nutrients and can be used by the body to promote cell health and break the vicious cycle of dysphoria.

If your cells are trying to live in a polluted environment, they cannot function properly to maintain the body/mind system at its peak. Besides nourishing brain cells and unclogging the metabolism that serves the brain, nutrients can actually boost your built-in pollution control mechanisms. In doing this, it can raise your energy level and produce an overall sense of well-being — body and mind. As your sense of well-being increases, your mind begins to produce more optimistic forecasts, which can be self-fulfilling and self-reinforcing. As your mental attitude becomes more positive, you are more likely to seek out and engage in what is good for you. This is the way to a cycle of ever-increasing well-being.

## HEALTHY CELLS DEMAND DAILY EXERCISE

Have you ever given thought to how your body rids itself of cell waste — called "toxins"? Would you be surprised if I told you it requires exercise for efficient removal of these products? Can you believe it when I tell you that without the removal of toxins from the cells, we would die within 24 hours?[12] Let me explain.

Almost all tissues of the body (you remember, tissues are simply structures made from similar cells to perform a specific purpose) drain excess fluid directly from the spaces between cells. If there were not a system provided for clearing this interstitial fluid, there would be "system-wide" swelling that would probably eventually lead to death.

We often see swelling at the ankles, under the eyes, and in other tissues. But nature, of course, knew that would happen before we did, so the perfect provision for elimination of all waste has been made. The route provided is called the lymphatic system and the fluid removed is called lymph.

The lymph contains plasma proteins and large particles of matter, neither of which are able to be removed by the blood. Bacteria, viruses, and other foreign matter are also filtered out and destroyed. This is done by a pumping action of the muscle fibers (a form of exercise) in the lymph vessel walls. The lymph is moved upward, never backward, by the pressure of skeletal muscle contraction as you move your body. So, there we have it — cell health through exercise.[13]

It is well documented that a few minutes a day on a trampoline, or a minimum of 30 minutes of very brisk walking, greatly stimulate the lymph nodes throughout the body to filter debris before they return to the bloodstream.

One simple conclusion to this healthy cell concept is: Those people who are "active," whether or not they have a specific exercise program, get rid of more cell debris (toxins) than those who live sedentary lives. **Therefore, if you are one who is always tired and lacks real zest for living, exercise the toxins out of your cells and feel the difference.**

## HEALTHY CELLS REQUIRE SPECIAL PROTECTION

The body's defense system is absolutely mind-boggling to think about. It has protected man for centuries from being annihilated in an unfriendly environment filled with many types of pathogenic (disease-producing) organisms. In addition, modern man is assaulted daily by impure water, impure air, chemically polluted soil, and a food chain filled with all kinds of cell health enemies. How have we been able to survive?

In the first place, **we were born with some very basic systems of protection — an army, a navy, and an air force of sorts.** Let's describe the "army" first. We'll say that it is our first line of defense.

The skin on the body is one of the major organs to serve as a defense against bacteria, viruses; and many organisms and chemicals could be very harmful to our system if they were permitted to enter. The skin doesn't even allow significant amounts of harmless substances, like water or air, to get inside. It is an effective cell protector. In addition, the skin produces small amounts of vitamin D and the male sex hormone, testosterone. Another helpful function of the skin is that it excretes a small amount of waste from the cells in the form of sweat. So, this is a highly valuable form of health defense.

Another part of this army to protect cell health is the system of mucous membranes that line the digestive, respiratory, urinary, and reproductive tracts. The mucous secreted by these protective membranes forms a wall around invaders that would destroy health, traps the offenders, and then destroys them. The mucus in the nose, for example, filters "tons" of potentially harmful substances and holds them trapped by the cilia (hair-like projections), and we are able to blow these from the nose passages. If they are swallowed instead, as sometimes is the case, the highly acidic juice of the stomach effectively puts any pathogens out of commission — forever.

A third form of defense by this army is the use of certain friendly bacteria that live in our intestines and produce some valuable protectors of cell health — the B-vitamins. These intestinal flora, as they are called, are still a mystery to medical science, but their beneficial qualities are neither doubted nor denied by them. What doctors often ignore is the fact that prescription drugs, which they so freely dispense, are destroyers of these wonderful defenders.

When the protection of the intestinal flora is lost, it is easy for the pathogenic bacteria to replace them in the gut and we can so easily become ill with disease. (Think about that when you so thoughtlessly swallow synthetic drugs!)

A fourth defender is provided by the tear glands. They keep the eyeballs moist and free from air pollutants as well as providing us the blessing of tears. Tears contain an enzyme which attacks the cell walls of bacteria and protects the eyes from invasion by these harmful enemies of the cells. Any person who has experienced "dry eyes" fully understands the benefits to eyeball cells when there is moisture present.

Now, let's turn our attention to the defenses supplied by our make-believe "navy." If some of our enemies were clever enough to

avoid death at the hand of our army's tactics, the second line of
defense is right there, ready for quick action. The navy's arsenal of
weapons is composed of a **higher-than-normal temperature
(fever), the lymphatic system, and phagocytes — a special kind of
fighter cells.**

Since the subjects of temperature and the lymphatic system have
already been covered in this chapter, and since the subject of phagocytes will be covered separately in the chapter on the immune system,
this is all to be said at this time. This navy, however, is an important part
of our cell defense system. We couldn't have healthy cells without it.

That brings us to the work of the body's make-believe "air force"
— our third source of protection for the body's cells. This defense
system is made up of chemicals — complex protein molecules which
are made by the body and are called antibodies. They are carried from
place to place in the body by the blood. They can destroy the toxins
produced by certain pathogens and can even destroy the pathogens
themselves. These micro-organisms are called antigens and the antibodies are produced by our air force in the thymus gland, the spleen,
and the lymph nodes. More about this will be discussed under the
subject of immunity in an upcoming chapter.

Before leaving the subject of cell protection, let me share a strong
conviction with you. If you are in good health and want to stay that
way, or if you are ill and want to get well, success in either of these
situations depends largely upon you — no one else can do it for you!

## THE BODY: A SELF-RESTORING SYSTEM

In summary, how does the body protect and repair itself, rejuvenate and rebuild tissues torn down through wear and tear of daily living? I believe it is done through using the same chemical elements
from which it was made — minerals, vitamins, enzymes, protein, carbohydrates, fats, and water. I do not believe it is accomplished
through drugs and man-made concoctions containing specific
amounts and types of unnatural elements. Nothing man can put
together in the way of magic formulas for health will ever heal or
rebuild or promote growth like the products provided for us by
nature.

**Yes, nature cures; nature heals; nature grows new cells, new
blood, new bones, new tissues, and all the rest.** It works slowly and
tediously, taking its time whether we like it or not. But, it works to
perfection. **Perfection is its goal. It believes in health** at its highest
and best. It just needs our cooperation in being positive, and patient!
We must believe it is working and that recovery is on the way.

## PROVIDE YOUR SYSTEM WITH THE BEST AND 'FEEL THE DIFFERENCE'

From all of this, you can certainly see the validity and the solidarity of the healthy cell concept. As you will learn from the testimonies in Chapter XII of this book, many people believe that the regular intake of dried barley juice has been effective in providing their cells the nutrients needed to move their whole body toward a vigorous and healthy lifestyle.

I encourage you to add it to your regular diet. You will feel the difference!

## WITHHOLD FROM YOUR SYSTEM THE WORST AND FEEL THE DIFFERENCE

It is safe to say that some of the worst foods include those high in saturated fats, high in sugar, man-made boxed and bottled concoctions and carbonated drinks. These are high on my list of foods to avoid.

But let me introduce a totally different idea under this heading: Withhold From Your System the Worst and Feel the Difference. That is, the subject of fasting.

It cannot be denied that fasting offers an incredible self-healing potential of the body. When done correctly, it is a powerful tool in the healing arsenal. It is both safe and effective as a means of helping the body to heal itself.

An M.D. friend whose specialty is operating a therapeutic fasting clinic says he has witnessed incredible healings of persons whose physicians had given up hope.

There is space for only one example. In a study of 156 people who collectively complained of symptoms from 31 medically diagnosed diseases (such things as ulcers, tumors, TB, sinusitis, Parkinson's disease, heart trouble, cancer, colitis, bronchitis, arthritis, etc.). 92% improved or totally recovered by fasting.

If you would like to pursue this treatment modality for poor health, write for my small booklet entitled "Fasting: The Physical and Spiritual Benefits" (see order form in back of book).

## CHAPTER V

# The Immune System: Your Personal 'Star Wars'

*by Susan C. Darbro*
*BA in English, BS in Nursing*

The immune system is extremely intricate and complex. It has been poorly understood, even by 20th century scientists with all of their advanced technological tools, until very recently. In the last 10 years, an explosion of new information has surfaced, bringing with it a new and deeper understanding of what the immune system is and how it works. According to one expert, "It is estimated that there is a flood of immunologic literature — about 7,000 articles appearing in 800 technical journals throughout the world each year."[1]

"So what?" you might be thinking. You must understand that your immune system is what protects you from invasion and infection. That is why I call it your personal "Star Wars."

Instead of starting out by talking about "polymorpho-nuclear leucocytes" and "enterochromaffin cells," let me simplify the concepts by telling you a little story. Pay close attention.

## A FAMILY REUNION

Grandpa Mac Forsythe was nearing his 75th birthday. He was a nice old man who liked everybody. His main pleasure in life was eating. He'd been the biggest eater in the whole town ever since anyone could remember. Folks said he was born hungry. He was just as happy with plain food as with fancy cooking, and there was nothing he didn't like. By the time he turned 70, he weighed almost 400 pounds!

Grandpa Mac lived with his wife Estelle in a big old house on Maple Street. (Estelle was a shriveled-up, bony old woman who was confined to a wheelchair, and no one paid her much attention.) The Forsythe home had been the talk of the town when it was new, but it was old now and had gradually fallen into serious disrepair — Grandpa Mac was too busy eating to paint the house or patch the roof!

Grandpa Mac and Estelle had two children, girls — Helga and Bea — and they had moved away years ago. Helga, the eldest, was as nice as she could be, except she loved to gossip. She also had a bad habit of being bossy, and, when there was a fight going on, she would always egg on the combatants. Helga was always on the go, her mouth going 90-miles-a-minute as well. When she was 16, she fell in love with a wild boy from the other side of the tracks, Nat Teasel. Everybody called him "N.K." N.K. was known for miles around for his bad reputation. He had a mean temper and a bad disposition. Some folks said he was a natural-born killer, which nearly broke his mother's heart (old Mrs. Teasel was a sweet old lady).

Well, Helga and N.K. ran off and got married. N.K. became a night watchman, and he and Helga had one child, a little boy named Preston. Preston, the poor little thing, was a quiet child who always tried to be the peacemaker in the family. When N.K. got into one of his tempers, Preston would cry and say, over and over again, "Please stop, Daddy." Mrs. Teasel came to live with them soon after Preston was born. She was a mild-mannered old woman who spent most of her time sitting in a rocking chair on the front porch reminiscing about her childhood.

Bea (her actual name was Beatrice Humor), Grandpa Mac's younger daughter, got married but couldn't have any children. One day she heard about a new treatment for her condition called "plasma cell therapy," and the next thing you know, she had four sets of triplets — Little Bea, Brenda, Bonnie, Benjamin, Bert, Beauford, Betty, Barbara, Billy, Brittany, Babette, and Butterball. Bea's children were a barrel of fun, but they were very mischievous. You could always find the little Humors making a mess in the kitchen, pretending to be conducting chemistry experiments. You could never be sure what they were up to.

Well, the whole family came to see Grandpa Mac and Estelle for Grandpa's birthday. The big old house on Maple Street was filled with laughter and noise.

Suddenly, there was a great crash, as part of the roof caved in. Grandpa Mac was sitting in his easy chair and noticed something purple amidst the chunks of fallen plaster and splintered wood. He immediately thought it was something to eat, so he rushed over and grabbed it. Everyone else stood by watching with saucer eyes — they'd never seen anything quite like it before and the crash had really frightened them. Suddenly, after Grandpa Mac had taken a couple of bites, Helga started screaming, "Oh my, oh my! It's a Martian! We've been invaded by Martians! Help! Help!" Sure enough, one by one in rapid succession the strange little purple things were dropping in through the gaping hole in the ceiling.

The whole house was immediately in an uproar. Little purple Martians were everywhere. N.K. came running in from the hallway brandishing his loaded pistol and started shooting the creatures. Grandpa Mac tripped over them and then ate them. Helga was running around, as usual, calling everyone to come and telling them what to do.

All of Bea's children rushed in from the kitchen carrying bowls and jars. Bonnie had a bottle of lye which she poured over one unfortunate Martian, causing its skin to bubble and melt away. Billy had a squirt-gun full of glue which he squirted all over a dozen Martians, hopelessly entangling them with each other. Butterball had the honey pot and kept dousing the creatures with honey, which made Grandpa Mac lunge for them because he loved honey so much.

Barbara, Bernice, Brittany, and Babette joined hands and formed a ring around Grandma Estelle, who didn't realize what was happening and couldn't defend herself. Soon, all the invaders were overcome. "Stop, stop," shouted Preston. "It's okay. You can quit. We're safe!"

The house was a mess, with dead Martians and debris everywhere. Helga gave orders to get out the vacuum and soon everything was swept away. What a day to remember!

When all the excitement was over, old Mrs. Teasel called them all together and told them the story of how robbers had once invaded her home. "Now children," she said, "You must always remember what happened today." "Don't worry," said little Bea, "I won't EVER forget!"

Now, I'm sure you must be wondering how in the world a silly story like this can help you understand the immune system, so I'll lose no time in explaining.

## RECOGNIZING THE INVADERS

The immune system protects the body from invasion, so our first question is, "How does the immune system know who and what is the enemy?" I chose purple Martians for my story, because the most important concept in understanding the bad guys is to understand the body sees them as foreign substances. **The body has the ability to recognize its own parts as "self" and other things as "nonself." Invaders are nonself,** and are usually referred to by the term antigen(s).

An antigen can be a virus, a bacterium, a fungus, or a parasite, or even a portion or product of one of these organisms. Tissues or cells from another individual, unless it is an identical twin, can also act as antigens. Because a transplanted organ is seen as "foreign," the body's natural response is to reject it. The body will even reject nourishing proteins unless they are first broken down, by the digestive system, into their primary building blocks.[2] Antigens such as viruses, bacteria, and fungi must penetrate healthy cells in order to reproduce. That is their goal, and that is what the immune system seeks to prevent.

## ELEMENTS OF IMMUNITY: THE SYSTEM

Now we know the enemy, let's unravel other elements in my little story. Each element corresponds to an element in our immune system. The old house on Maple Street is our body. Houses take a great deal of upkeep and so do we. Grandpa Mac didn't take good care of his house, and it caved in. When we fail to take good care of our bodies by neglecting to practice good health habits — proper diet, adequate rest, and regular exercise — we do the same thing. To have strong and healthy immune systems, we need strong, healthy bodies to house them in.

## THE STRUCTURES

It might be good to stop for a minute and clarify something at this point. Many organ systems in the body — your urinary tract or digestive tract, for instance — are interconnected and function in a logical, progressive order just like the plumbing in a house. The immune system, however, is not like that. Different parts of it are found here, there, and everywhere in our bodies.

Immune system tissues are called "lymphoid tissues." They include the tonsils and adenoids in your neck, the thymus gland in your chest, the spleen in the left side of your abdomen, the appendix in the right side of your abdomen, the bone marrow inside the long bones of your body, the lymph nodes scattered throughout your body, and various blood and tissue cells which are just about everywhere at once.

Also included in this is your "lymphatic system" — a network of drainage vessels which parallels the bloodstream, vital to the functioning of the immune system.

Like a system of small creeks and streams that empty into larger and larger rivers, the vessels of the lymphatic network merge into increasingly larger tributaries. At the base of the neck, the large lymphatic ducts empty into the bloodstream.[3]

**Our bodies are specially constructed to resist disease,** just like a stone wall or high fence keeps strangers out of a house. Our first line of defense is our skin, which we can think of as a protective coating or shell for our body. It is specially equipped with secretions of fatty acids that have a deadly effect on certain microorganisms.[4] Unless we damage it by some kind of injury, it is sufficient to keep most would-be invaders out.

The size of the invader is of little importance, because tiny invaders can be just as deadly as those we can see. The AIDS virus, for example, is so small that 230 million of them could fit in a space no bigger than the period at the end of this sentence.[5] This means a tiny scratch or pinprick can have fatal consequences, and it is important for you to keep wounds clean and covered, particularly when you are around someone who is sick.

Another one of the custom-made features we have at our disposal is in the respiratory tract — tiny hair-like projections lining the respiratory tract, which trap foreign bodies and prevent them from lodging inside cells, where they can begin to grow and multiply. In addition, special linings of our respiratory and digestive tracts called mucous membranes ooze out a thick, sticky substance which also traps invaders. Special enzymes found in tears and saliva are harmful to many organisms, just in case we get some in our eyes or mouth. Many body fluids, including blood, also contain chemical substances to counteract an attack by antigens.

## FAMILY PORTRAITS: THE MACROPHAGE

Let's move from the house to the family. You will remember Grandpa Mac Forsythe was the first character in my story. His real name is **macrophage**, and he represents a **large, specialized cell, whose job it is to engulf and consume foreign substances.** A macrophage is one type of phagocyte, which engulfs and digests invaders. What this means to us is that if we get caught sitting next to someone who sneezes, a macrophage in our body would come along and see that the sneezed particles were "nonself" and immediately try to consume them before they could reach the safety of the interior of a cell. (That is assuming those hair-like projections failed to trap the particles in the nose and windpipe.) Phagocytes, of which Grandpa Mac is one type, are an extremely important part of our immune system.

## THE STEM CELL

Grandpa Mac's elderly wife Estelle represents a mother stem cell. **Stem cells produce baby fighter cells** which travel to other parts of the body to mature. If they mature in bone marrow, they become "B cells," whereas, if they go through the thymus gland, they become "T cells." Stem cells do not themselves participate directly in an immune attack, but they produce the fighter cells who do.

The immune defense system is often divided into two categories, something like the army and the navy. One part is called "humoral," which I represented by Beatrice Humor and all her children. The other division is called cellular or "cell-mediated," which was Helga and her family in our story.

## THE T-CELL FAMILY

Let's review Helga Teasel and her family first. Helga's real name would be helper T cell, which means she was born of a mother stem cell and migrated early in life to the thymus gland, where she "grew up." There are several types of T cells (technically, they are "T lymphocytes") **a helper T cell is one which turns T cells and B cells on.** This is why we saw Helga running around shouting orders and agitating everyone on the scene.

Another type of T cell is the suppressor T cell, which was Preston Teasel in our story. **A suppressor T cell's job is to call off the fight** after an immune response has successfully repelled an invasion. Yet another type of T cell is the natural killer cell (remember N.K. Teasel?), **which attacks and destroys other cells by puncturing their cell membranes.** Killer cells will attack our own body cells if they have been taken over by antigens. N.K. was a night watchman to illustrate the fact that killer cells prowl around our bodies looking for abnormalities, like cancer cells, and destroy them.

There are many more kinds of T lymphocytes in the ranks of our immune system, but these three represent the major types of fighter cells. One additional job they have is to produce chemicals harmful to antigens. T cells make lymphokines, "diverse and potent chemicals that can call into play many other cells and substances...,"[6] among which is the substance interferon you may have read about. So much for Helga's side of the family.

## THE HUMORAL DIVISION

The humoral division of the immune system is represented in my story by Bea and her children, namely B cells. B cells (actually B lymphocytes), you will remember, are born of a mother stem cell and then mature in bone marrow. **The main job of a B cell is to secrete substances called antibodies** (represented by Bea's numerous children in the story). Antibodies are like snowflakes or fingerprints in that each one is different, made for one specific antigen. There are thousands, or millions, of antigens out there, and our body has the capacity to make antibodies to fit each one, just as a key fits in a lock. "By storing just a few cells specific for each potential invader, it (our body) has room for the entire army."[7] Thus, "The immune system stockpiles a tremendous arsenal ...."[8]

## PROLIFERATING ANTIBODIES

**When an antigen appears, the B cell that matches it swells into what is called a "plasma cell"** (remember Bea's treatment for infertility?) **and begins to rapidly reproduce antibodies.** As Dr. Michael Weiner puts it, "When a particular antigen presents itself, cells specifically matched to it are stimulated to multiply into a whole army."[9] Many B cells are unable to recognize the foreign body until a macrophage displays partially digested antigen on its surface, which is why Helga was calling Bea and her children to come only after Grandpa Mac had taken bites out of the first little Martian.

Antibodies do not all function alike. Some, like Bonnie and her bottle of lye, cause invaders to dissolve. Others, like Billy and his glue gun, change the surface of the antigens so they clump together, making it impossible for them to function. Clumping also makes it easier for macrophages and other scavenger cells to find and digest them. Other antibodies, like Butterball and his honey pot, coat the antigens to make them attractive to phagocytes. Still others cover them with poisonous protein which renders the antigens harmless. And, like Barbara, Bernice, Brittany, and Babette, some surround an area and cordon it off.

According to one expert, the body may have more than a million kinds of B cells, each producing a different antibody.[10] I need to clarify one part of my story here. B cells make only one type of antibody each. So, Bea would have only had 12 "Little Beas," not 12 different children. I like what Dr. Weiner says about the variety of immune responses:

> *The components of the immune system are organized and inter-connected in such a way as to permit a remarkable flexibility of response. Rarely is your body limited to just one way of dealing with the challenge presented by an antigen. If one defense strategy does not work, your immune system is ready with another.*[11]

## MEMORY CELLS

Remember old Mrs. Teasel, who sat around remembering days gone by? At the end of the story, she was exhorting Little Bea to remember the Martian invasion. Mrs. Teasel represents a **T memory cell** and Little Bea represents a **B memory cell,** both of which have "photographic" memories of invaders and can program the body to make antibodies against them at the drop of a hat. Memory cells live for years, and it is because of them that people who come down with measles at age two will never get them again, in spite of the fact that they are exposed time and time again over the years.

## THE LYMPHATIC DUCT SYSTEM

The other element in my story which needs explanation is the vacuum cleaner, which is the lymphatic duct system:

> *The lymph nodes are connected by a network of vessels that receive drainage from the organs associated with the nodes and from throughout the body. **This Lymphatic duct system serves as both the information network and the transportation complex** for your body's defense personnel. In areas where there is no direct lymphatic drainage, lymphatic materials are transported by the blood. The lymph nodes contain specialized compartments — some containing B cells, some with T cells, and some containing macrophages. Webbed areas in the lymph nodes trap antigens and filter them out of the clear lymphatic fluid, or lymph.*[12]

All of this is only a tiny scratch on the surface of the immune system, but I hope it helps you to better understand and appreciate your body.

[Note: For any of you who are interested in learning more on this subject, I recommend *Maximum Immunity* by Michael A. Weiner, Ph.D., and for superb photographs, the June 1986 issue of *National Geographic Magazine.*]

## KEEPING YOUR IMMUNE SYSTEM FIT
## THROUGH NUTRITION

Well, you may be asking, what does all of this have to do with the green leaves of barley, anyway? I know you've heard it before, but what you assimilate from what you eat is what you are. If you feed your body the right stuff, it will work for you, and if you don't, it won't.

Some of our favorite foods literally paralyze our immune system. Here is a good example: A recent discovery is that **sugar decreases our body's ability to destroy bacteria — it destroys our immune system!**[13]

There are nine teaspoons of sugar in one 12-ounce Coke. This means if you drink three Cokes (or other soft drinks) in one day, you have immobilized 92 percent of your defense troops!

### TABLE 3

| DAILY SUGAR INTAKE (TEASPOONS) | NUMBER OF BACTERIA EACH WHITE BLOOD CELL DESTROYS IN 30 MINUTES | DECREASE IN EFFICIENCY |
|:---:|:---:|:---:|
| 0 | 14 | — |
| 6 | 10 | 25% |
| 12 | 6 | 60% |
| 18 | 2 | 85% |
| 24 | 1 | 92% |

I'd sure hate to let a cancer cell get past my immune system just because I decided to have some pie a la mode one day, wouldn't you? Sugar isn't the only culprit. Examine these quotes from Dr. Weiner's book:

*"Our food, water, and air have steadily become contaminated with the heavy metals — lead, cadmium, and mercurys. In animal studies, these metals suppress all aspects of immune functions, reducing cell-mediated and humoral immunity, depressing phago-cyte responses, and increasing susceptibility to infection (Gordon 1983).*

*"A major source of cadmium is cigarette smoke .... Organic fer-tilizers made from sewage sludge often lead to dangerous cadmium*

*levels in produce. Elevated cadmium levels have been shown to impair host resistance, antibody response, B and T cell response, and phagocyte response (Beisel 1982) and to depress bone morrow function (Weiner 1981).* [14]

*"It is now clear that high dietary fat intake can seriously impair immune functioning."* [15]

*"Macrophages with a high level of cholesterol show a decrease in phagocytic ability. Some studies also suggest that high dietary cholesterol may diminish cell-mediated and humoral immunity."* [16]

*"A high-fat diet leads to elevated levels of bile acids in the colon. These break down into deoxycholic acids, which are dangerous carcinogens ... cancer of the breast, pancreas, gallbladder, ovary, uterus and prostate, as well as leukemia, are all positively correlated with a diet high in animal protein fat and cholesterol .... High-fat diets and obesity also correlate strongly with the incidence, tumor size and speed of development of breast cancer (deWaard 1982)."* [17]

## GREEN BARLEY: IMMUNE SYSTEM SUPPORT

The question arises, "How can we help our immune system?" Barley juice is a good source of vitamin A, which "has long been known to promote nonspecific resistance to a wide variety of pathogens ...."[18] Weiner goes on to say:

*"By helping to preserve the integrity of skin and mucous membranes, vitamin A helps to maintain the protective barriers against infectious organisms entering the body. Vitamin A is also needed for the production of bacteria-fighting Iysozymes in tears, saliva and sweat (Rosenbaum 1984).*

*"... Studies of animals with vitamin A deficiency have shown atrophy of thymus and Iymphoid tissues, decrease in total number of T and B cells, and depression of T cell response to . . . infectious agents."* [19]

An article appearing in the *Journal of the American Medical Association (JAMA)* agrees, "Modest increases in dietary vitamin A enhance resistance to infection in animals...."[20]

Barley juice is a wonderful source of vitamin $B_1$, which mildly enhances the immune system. When it is deficient in the diet, the size of lymphatic organs grows smaller and the number of T and B cells decreases.[21]

Vitamin $B_2$, called riboflavin, is found in large amounts in barley juice. Riboflavin is an immunity promoter and is involved in the production of antibodies. Deficiencies are linked to decreases in antibody response, lymphatic organ size and total number of T and B cells in the blood.[22]

Vitamin $B_6$, or pyridoxine, which is also plentiful in barley juice, "seems to be the most important for proper immune functioning with deficiencies causing more serious immune problems than with the other B vitamins."[23] The researchers in the *JAMA* article also found that "volunteers with short-term experimental $B_6$ deficiencies could not react properly to vaccines."[24]

The same article points out that, "folic acid deficiency depresses immune functions in both animals and man."[25] It goes on to say that the lack of folic acid causes lymphoid tissue to waste away, as well as fighter cells to diminish in number. Weiner points out that lack of folic acid also causes the body to let tumors grow more easily.[26] There is good news for you, however. Barley juice is high in folic acid!

Choline is another ingredient found in barley juice which is good for your immune system. Without it, the humoral immune division (Bea and her children) do not function properly. This is especially true when dietary lack occurs during pregnancy, according to animal experiments.[27]

Vitamin C is another important element in the smooth functioning of our immune system. The JAMA researchers tell us that besides helping the phagocytes (Grandpa Mac's family) get from where they are to where they are needed, vitamin C also influences the killing functions of fighter cells. You should also note that:

> *Aspirin has an anti-vitamin C effect, promoting the loss of vitamin C through the urine and also decreasing uptake of the vitamin by white blood cells. Taking aspirin also seems to increase the danger of a spreading viral infection ... For these reasons, you may want to think twice before taking aspirin along with vitamin C for your cold or flu.* [28]

One interesting fact I gleaned from my study of the immune system is that vitamin D, which our bodies make themselves, can actually suppress immune functioning. Guess what — barley juice doesn't have any! Of course, any fat-soluble vitamin can build up in the body and cause problems if you take too much over a long period of time. So, be careful with your supplements, particularly if you are faithful in taking dried barley juice.

Minerals are also necessary for the proper functioning of our immune system. "Copper deficiency has been linked to lower resistance."[29] Barley juice is a good source of copper! Iron, also contained in barley juice, is necessary, although, once again, caution should be used in taking iron supplements because too much iron is just as dangerous to our bodies as not enough. Iron is necessary to get oxygen to the cells, and the cells of the immune system have a "relatively high" oxygen requirement.[30] The JAMA researchers also point out that iron deficiency makes lymphoid tissue waste away and causes "defective macrophage and neutrophil functions."[31] Zinc, abundant in barley juice, "is an extremely important immune stimulant, specifically promoting T cell immunity."[32] Helga and her family need it. Without zinc, the activity of killer cells is lower, antibodies do not function well, and the growth of stem cells in the thymus gland is adversely affected.[33]

This all boils down to one thing — **if we want to keep healthy, we must keep our immune system functioning in tip-top condition. Barley juice is full of vitamins and minerals that the immune system needs.** So, it follows that one of the best ways we can help ourselves remain free of disease is to drink dried barley juice on a regular basis.

## CHAPTER VI

# Meet Your Friend: Chlorophyll

*by Susan C. Darbro*
*BA in English, BS in Nursing*

If you're like me, the word "chlorophyll" probably triggers a subconscious flashback. You are in a hot and stuffy science classroom decorated with periodic charts of the elements on the walls. An overwhelming feeling of boredom and cabin fever engulfs you as you patiently wait for the bell to ring, freeing you from the awful lecture on photosynthesis. Well, guess what! You weren't really saved by the bell after all — here it comes again! I'll try and make it as simple as possible, but in order to appreciate the power barley juice has to improve your health, you must understand a little about chlorophyll, and in order to understand chlorophyll, we need to review photosynthesis.

## A SCIENCE LESSON

The thing that gives barley juice its green color is chlorophyll, a pigment found in all plants. It manifests itself in different but chemically related groups — chlorophyll-a, chlorophyll-b, etc. The great majority of chlorophyll is in the form of chlorophyll-a, found in all "oxygen evolving" organisms. So, we will ignore the other chlorophylls, leaving them happily undisturbed amidst brown algae and other lower forms of plant life.

As you know, plants do not eat eggs for breakfast, or lunch at McDonald's in order to get food for energy. They must make their own sugars and starches using only air, water, and sunshine. The recipe is quite long and involved, and our friend chlorophyll is a major ingredient. Chlorophyll molecules act as tiny but powerful antennae to absorb light and transfer it to other chlorophyll molecules which undergo chemical oxidation, converting light into chemical energy the plant can use.

Photosynthesis is the process by which the plant takes carbon dioxide from the air, water from the soil, and light energy from the sun and puts them all together to use for its growth and maintenance. The important thing to remember is that photosynthesis would be impossible without chlorophyll.

This makes chlorophyll a very important substance to you and me. **If there were no chlorophyll, there would be no photosynthesis. If there were no photosynthesis, there would be no plant life. Without plants, there could be no animal life on earth, including us!** Chlorophyll, therefore, is absolutely essential to life.

## A HISTORY LESSON

Historically, chlorophyll has generated interest for a long time. In 1844, a scientist named Verdeil noted chlorophyll and red blood pigment reacted similarly when tested with acid compounds,[1] but it was not until 1913 that the precise molecular structure of chlorophyll was identified by German scientist Richard Willstatter.[2] At the same time, a Swiss doctor, E. Buergi, discovered **chlorophyll stimulates growth of human tissues**.[3] By 1930, enough interest had been generated about chlorophyll to establish the Foundation for the Study of Chlorophyll and Photosynthesis at Antioch College in Ohio.

Around this time, Dr. Hans Fischer, who had won a Nobel Prize in 1931 for research on red blood pigment, announced he had been using chlorophyll in the treatment of his patients with what he called, "promising" results.[4] Also around this time, Philadelphia's Temple University Department of Experimental Pathology took up the challenge. It created medicinal solutions and ointments made from the extraction of chlorophyll from nettles.

Patients at Temple University Hospital were then treated with the chlorophyll medicines under carefully controlled conditions.[5] This resulted in the granddaddy of therapeutic chlorophyll studies, authored by Benjamin Gruskin, M.D., director of Experimental Pathology and Oncology at Temple University.

His study involved not only his own handiwork, but also that of 19 of his distinguished colleagues, and had a data base of 1,200 patients. This report made its appearance in July, 1940, in the *American Journal of Surgery*. It sparked a huge interest in further study and practical application of chlorophyll in many areas.

By 1952, chlorophyll was not so much a scientific subject of investigation as a cure-all by international popular demand. The business world took over its use, leaving more conservative and methodical scientists behind in a cloud of green dust.

### CHLOROPHYLL WARS

In 1951, more than 40 American companies were pushing chlorophyll products and doing a $22 million-a-year business[6] — quite a large sum of money back then. Besides medicinal products, chlorophyll was added to over 150 commodities, including toilet tissue, mouthwash, hair restorers, antacid tablets, chewing gum, breath sweeteners, toothpastes, stick deodorants, shampoos, reducing pills, air purifiers, foot pads and powders, colognes, aftershave lotions, pillows, cleansing cream, bubble baths, cough drops, cigarettes and tobacco, dog food, and even chlorophyll-treated crib sheets!

The package label of one Australian product called "SOBER Tablets" read, for "relief of symptoms of the after-effects of drinking alcohol; symptomatic relief of hangover, nausea, and vomiting." Its media advertisements were reported to have said SOBER Tablets actually neutralized the inebriating effects of alcohol.[7] Another favorite of mine is a product containing aspirin and chlorophyll advertised as being "for a stinking headache."[8] As one writer put it, "A number of chlorophyll products were obviously born in over-imaginative sales departments."[9]

Proponents and skeptics waged chlorophyll wars for a time, each claiming victory. The deodorant power of chlorophyll was a central issue for debate and makes interesting reading. Here is an example. Compare the following sets of excerpts:

*"There is now no doubt a sufficient concentration of chlorophyllin greatly reduces breath odors due to traces of food in the mouth. Investigators in many laboratories, including two testing laboratories well known for their hard-boiled attitude toward commercial products, have mixed the green tablets with pungent substances ranging from crushed onion and garlic to benzyl mercaptan, the essence of skunk, and ethyl mercaptan, the odorous chemical added to cooking gas to warn of leaks. In all cases, the odor disappeared and the test tubes remained free of odor for some time thereafter.*

*A 'chlorophyll' tablet slowly dissolved in the mouth, in most cases likewise eliminated breath odors caused by eating onions, drinking alcohol or ingesting other strong-smelling substances.*

*In addition, the green tablets may diminish body and menstrual odors. 'I know of no scientifically controlled tests of this so far.' an authority I interviewed declared, 'and I am still unconvinced. Still, some of the results are impressive. I wouldn't want to say there's nothing to it.'*

*Dr. Westcott himself reports a single tablet taken in the morning reduced perspiration odors throughout the day in 67 patients and experimental subjects.*

*Dr. Frederick S. Tablor of New Jersey, found that the green pills abolished menstrual odors in more than half of a group of women patients.*

*Dr. Harry E. Tebrock, medical director of the Sylvania Electric Corporation, says that the tablets eliminated body and other personal odors in more than 80 percent of 584 Sylvania factory employees."*[10]

The most recent dissent and in some respects the most remarkable, comes from *Good Housekeeping* magazine, which, in its August 1952 issue, expressed skepticism, if not contempt, for claims being made for chlorophyll products. *Good Housekeeping* did "a certain amount of breath checking on test groups using various (chlorophyll dentifrice) products."

The article concluded:

*"As you know, the habit of brushing the teeth with a good dentifrice after eating is in itself an excellent method of controlling mouth odor. So far, we have been unable to determine whether the results we obtained should be credited to a good toothpaste formula or to the chlorophyll"*

As for perspiration odor, *Good Housekeeping* reported, "for a week 50 women took these (chlorophyll) tablets for us, meanwhile using no underarm deodorant. The pills did not work ...."[11]

Or, how about these two:

*"In any case, chlorophyll ... probably has none of the deodorizing or other remarkable properties credited to it. If it did, horses, cattle, and spinach eaters would all have sweet breaths.*[12]

*I have put the power of chlorophyll to a stern test on a dog. In what should have been a contented old age, Duke, our 170 pound Great Dane, had fallen upon evil days. He loved all of us and all of our friends. Why was it nobody wanted him to come near for his customary hello? You could see the puzzled hurt in his gold-brown eyes. His teeth and diet had every attention, yet daily the poor dog became more unbearable.*

*An enormous brute, it took a lot of chlorophyll to turn the trick, but six of the green tablets daily cleared his breath completely. This was Duke's special legacy to dogdom and to all who do not want to get rid of their dogs because of intolerable B.O. or halitosis.*

*Our experience has now been duplicated by Dr. Maurice E. Serling of Larchmont, N.Y. From Cocker Spaniels to Borzois — all patients in his veterinary hospital — the doctor abolished B.O. and halitosis within six hours after giving the green medicine. When the tablets were withdrawn, the evil condition returned within 24 hours. When treatment was resumed, it vanished again![13]*

## WILL THE REAL FACTS PLEASE STAND UP?

One reason for the apparent lack of uniformity of opinion was the failure of the chlorophyll industry to standardize the type and quality of chlorophyll and the chlorophyll derivatives it used. Scientific research on chlorophyll in the arena of medicine involved then, as now, mostly two types. One is chlorophyll-a, which is chemically structured so that it doesn't dissolve in water. Early researchers believed that the chlorophyll found in nature, therefore, was of little practical use. As late as 1958, one noted physician, Dr. H.R. Wetherell, of the University of Nebraska College of Medicine, warned his patients:

*"We do not wish to imply that eating large quantities of vegetables rich in chlorophyll, such as spinach and beet greens, is good for one's heart. The materials we have studied are derived from chlorophyll which has been subjected to several complicated laboratory procedures."[14]*

Newer research, however, substantiates the fact that raw, naturally occurring chlorophyll is absorbed in the intestines, following the same pathway that digestion of vitamin A takes.[15] Natural chlorophyll would be much better absorbed were it not encased in plant fiber. **One advantage green barley powder has over fresh vegetables in this regard is that, because its fiber is removed, its chlorophyll is very easily digested.**

Since early researchers were unaware of these facts, they devised a way to make natural chlorophyll in a water-soluble form. Over 800 chlorophyll derivatives were experimented with, but by far the most useful and significant are the "chlorophyllins."[16] These are made by chemically removing the side chains of the chlorophyll molecule and, in many instances, changing the center atom from magnesium to a different metal, usually copper or iron. While it is true that "eating large quantities of vegetables rich in chlorophyll is not the same as treating laboratory animals with chlorophyll derivatives,"[17] both naturally occurring chlorophyll and its chlorophyllin derivatives have immense therapeutic value. Let's go back and dig a little deeper into the research done before the commercial explosion of chlorophyll products got out of hand.

## BLOOD RELATIVES

One of the most fascinating discoveries in the biological sciences was the observation of the similarity between the green pigment in plants and the red pigment in blood. They are nearly identical. The major difference is that the central atom in chlorophyll is magnesium, whereas the central atom in hemoglobin is iron. What is the significance? To me, it seems clear that the pigment chlorophyll is the "blood" of plants, and the fact it bears such a striking resemblance to the oxygen carrying pigment coloring our blood is no idle curiosity.

One of the first to see this connection was Dr. Hans Fischer, who used it in the treatment of anemic patients.[18] Researchers saw that the similarity between chlorophyll and hemoglobin went one step further — both remained nearly identical during breakdown processes. In the Antioch studies, partially digested grass was being used for chlorophyll breakdown study. Lois Miller in the *Science News Letter* says of this work; And when this partly digested food was fed to rats, **"it directly stimulated formation of red blood cells."**[19]

Modern-day researchers tend to pooh-pooh the idea that the blood of plants can become the blood of humans, but I, for one, disagree. Even scientists admit in a very scholarly article that, "Despite these variations in structure and function, evidence suggests porphyrin biosynthesis (generation of respiratory pigment: hemoglobin, the blood of humans and animals, chlorophyll in plants) is essentially similar in all biological systems."[20]

## CHLOROPHYLL THE HEALER

Dr. Gruskin repeated the observation made earlier by Swiss researcher Buergi when, after using chlorophyll and its derivatives on 1,200 patients, he found chlorophyll has a "stimulating effect upon the growth of supportive connective tissue cells and development of granulation tissue."[21] This has enormous significance in medicine, especially in the field of surgery, because **the body must repair itself**

**and chlorophyll helps it to do so.** "Granulation tissue" is the early, grainy cells which appear on the surface of wounds during healing. Drs. Buergi and Gruskin showed, in a nutshell, that chlorophyll speeds up the process!

Fifteen years later, further research done by Drs. Sack and Barnard, published in the *New York State Medical Journal*, postulates a reason for this phenomenon; that the application of **chlorophyllins increases local blood supply.**[22] Since blood supplies the nutrients and oxygen which cells need to reproduce, greater blood supply means greater healing power.

Another reason for the acceleration of the healing process suggested by the Sack and Barnard research is that, when a wound becomes inflamed, the red blood cells become clumped together and are, therefore, unable to work efficiently. Their studies suggest that chlorophyll has an "inhibitory effect" on clumping, or "hemagglutination" as it is called in medical jargon. Here is what they concluded:

*"That the healing process resulted directly from application of chloresium ointment is indicated by the fact that all of the ulcerations had been previously resistant to other therapy, and, while bacterially sterile prior to the initiation of the study, had showed no evidence of an active healing process. That the healing process resulted specifically from chlorophyllin's effect on the character of the wound exudate (drainage) is suggested, if not proved, by the fact that the hemagglutinative and inflammatory properties of the exudates could be uniformly reduced by chlorophyllin in vitro (in a test tube). This argues against any conclusion that the change in the character of the wound exudate was the result rather than the cause of the healing progress."*[23]

Wound healing is important in the medical world in fields other than surgery. Backing up again to 1940, a dermatologist in the Temple University Hospital study reported using "chlorophyll in ointment form in treatment of various skin conditions and found it particularly helpful in chronic ulcers ...." Ear, nose, and throat specialists used chlorophyll on patients with chronic sinus infections, resulting in "a final cure of all former symptoms." The conclusion of ear, nose, and throat experiments is that "it is interesting to note that there is not a single case recorded in which either improvement or cure has not taken place."[24]

## CHLOROPHYLL AND INFECTION

Gruskin and associates treated a whole host of conditions, including open wounds, infections in deep surgical wounds, fistulas (abnormal drainage tracts communicating within the body) of the abdomen and chest, emphysema (pus in the lungs), abscesses of the liver and kidney, rectal lesions, leg ulcers due to poor circulation, brain abscesses, gangrenous appendicitis, and uterine cancer. He says, "From this partial list of cases, it becomes apparent **the use of chlorophyll in any acute or chronic suppurative (containing pus) process has resulted in definite improvement.**"[25] Chlorophyll has the ability to break down carbon dioxide and release oxygen, which spells disaster for many bacteria that thrive in deep wounds away from air.

Gruskin and his associates were not the only ones to come up with these results. Dr. Lawrence Smith, in his article, "The Present Status of Topical Chlorophyll Therapy," states: "What was of greatest importance in the decade following the issuing of the Temple University report was the almost universal corroboration of the original findings."[26]

An easy-to-read sample of these comes from the October 1952 issue of *Science Digest*:

*"Drs. Michael Weingarten and Benjamin Payson, of Beth Israel Hospital, New York, and other groups of surgeons found 'chlorophyll' tablets deodorized patients with colostomies (artificial openings in the lower intestine near the rectum) and enabled them to resume normal lives.*

*Dr. Earnest B. Carpenter of the Veterans Administration found chlorophyllin dressings deodorized and speeded the healing of stubborn osteomyelitis bone infections. Dr.'s Goldberg of Chicago obtained prompt healing in a wide variety of mouth infections.*

*Dr. Lewis J. Pollock and his associates at the Hines, IL, Veterans Hospital, found chlorophyllin preparations the most effective of 11 different agents in healing bed sores, a difficult problem in paralyzed patients In Australia, Dr. Henry Haughton obtained rapid **healing of severe burns** with the green dressings."*[27]

## BENEFITS OF CHLOROPHYLL THERAPY

Dr. Smith's review article in the July, 1950, issue of the *New York State Medical Journal*, has the best overall summary of the benefits of chlorophyll therapy I have come across. I would like to include a little of it for you to read:

"*Absence of toxicity has been another outstanding feature throughout more than a decade of clinical use, and agreement on the following clinical opinions is common to the reports.*

*1. 'Chlorophyll,' whether in the form of ointment or solution, promotes the growth of healthy granulation tissue.*

*2. It is conducive to the production of a clean granulating wound base.*

*3. Itching, pain, and local irritation, which so frequently are outstanding symptoms associated with ulcers, burns, wounds, and dermatoses, are usually relieved promptly, and the relief is gratefully acknowledged by the patient.*

*4. Normal repair and epithelization (new tissue, as in ulcer healing) proceeds more rapidly under 'chlorophyll' treatment of burns and dermatoses than with other agents. Malodorous (foul smelling) lesions are deodorized (an action not to be confused with mere contact deodorization as implied by certain less accurate promotional claims in some instances).*

*5. Blandness of action, freedom from tissue damage, and lack of toxicity as well as comforting, soothing relief are almost invariably characteristic of chlorophyll treatment.*" [28]

## CHLOROPHYLL STACKS UP

One more extremely interesting fact I'd like to share with you from Dr. Smith's paper is how chlorophyll stacked up against other remedies of the time. He quotes a study which employed sulfa drugs, penicillin, and vitamin D ointment against chlorophyll, and the chlorophyll won by a "much higher" score! [29]

World War II had provided the perfect laboratory for a life and-death test of the power of chlorophyll to aid in the healing process and to test the accuracy of Gruskin's work. An account to the public from *Reader's Digest* went like this:

"*... Dr. Warner F. Bowers and his associates at a U.S. Army general hospital during the war applied chlorophyll ointments and wet dressings to the stinking, wide-open wounds of boys lying in wards, so smelly that not only the victims but even the doctors and nurses lost their appetites. For strict scientific comparison, the doctors put chlorophyll dressings on one wounded soldier, left the next one without them, and so on. Amazingly, within 48 hours all odor faded away from the victims who had chlorophyll dressings.*

*Then, the untreated boys set up a holler. 'Give us the green medicine, too,' they begged. And the last trace of stench vanished from the osteomyelitis and fracture wards of the hospital.*" [30]

Dr. Bowers stated that he believed chlorophyll therapy was responsible for saving several limbs from amputation.[31] That's a pretty powerful recommendation.

## WHAT'S NEW IN CHLOROPHYLL RESEARCH?

Since 1955, little clinical research on chlorophyll has been done in this country. In 1960, an article was published by Dr. Leo Siegel in *Gastroenterology*, which reported a study at Presbyterian Hospital in Newark, NJ. Some excerpts from its summary are as follows:

*"... In 14 of 15 cases control of odor was either complete or wholly satisfactory to the patient and to those close to him .... Colostomy patients were more prone to have complete control of odor than those with ileostomies. However, the latter as a group had very satisfactory results ....*

*Definite toxicity or side reactions were not encountered....Such a preparation as the high potency chlorophyll tablet discussed here should help to make life much less trying for the patient and his family."[32]*

Twenty years later, the medical world was still trying to make sure chlorophyll works, as is illustrated by the publication of an article in the *Journal of the American Geriatrics Society*. Can you guess the result?

The study involved 62 female patients in a geriatric nursing home, and chlorophyllin successfully controlled body and fecal odors in 85 percent of those patients. This study also said the **chlorophyllin helped combat constipation as well as relieved gas discomfort in 50 percent of those same patients**, adding "the magnitude of the favorable estimates was impressive in a group of patients whose bowel difficulties were otherwise not readily manageable."[33] As late as 1983 they are still at it. An article published in *Drug Intelligence and Clinical Pharmacy*, reports that "There seems to be a trend for chlorophyllin efficacy in decreasing urinary odor."[34]

A study appearing in *Obstetrics and Gynecology* in 1968, recommended that lymph nodes be stained with chlorophyll so that they would be easily seen and therefore not missed by doctors who read X-rays or surgeons removing cancerous lymph nodes.[35]

The 1970s viewed chlorophyll as a possibility in the treatment of acute pancreatitis, a very nasty disease in which the pancreas eats itself up, so to speak. An article published in *Digestive Diseases*,[36] as well as one published in the *Archives of Pathological Laboratory Medicine* agreed that chlorophyllin was helpful — "Animals treated with ... injections of chlorophyll showed higher survival rate than in untreated controls."[37] However, a dissenting article appeared in *Annals of Surgery*. It is my feeling that the negative article failed to demonstrate a positive result because the pancreatitis in that research was induced in experimental animals by malnutrition.[38] The rats were in such poor overall health to begin with that even with chlorophyll they could not overcome such a serious disease. Of course, all three studies were strictly animal experiments, and, though it is my opinion that we can gain general human application from them, it is not strictly scientific to say so.

Chlorophyll studies in the 1980's seem to center on its use in the treatment of kidney stones. Two articles appearing in *Investigative Urology* agree that **soluble chlorophyllin both retards the growth of crystals (kidney "stones" are really crystals) and prolongs the time it takes for them to get started**.[39] In typical medical skeptic fashion, they conclude, "soluble chlorophyllin could be of clinical significance in calcium oxalate urolithiasis."[40] A third article on this subject was published in *Urological Research* and agreed, "Data obtained suggests chlorophyllin might be useful in treatment of calcium oxalate stone disease."[41] That should certainly interest those of you who have problems with kidney stones!

I hope after wading through all of this (and if you think this is bad, you should try and read some of these professional journal articles firsthand!), you can agree with me that **chlorophyll is just as much a "wonder drug" as the man-made wonder drugs of this century**. Green barley juice has oodles of easily digestible chloro phyll in it. As previously mentioned, the chlorophyll in green barley is so "alive" that it will photosynthesize. That's why I believe it is a food with REAL power.

Because I believe that the research that produced negative results was poorly done, and because of the continued clinical success in the use of chlorophyll for a myriad of health problems, **I can now state my firm belief in the healing power of chlorophyll. If chlorophyll were patentable, in my opinion it would be a widely used product by the medical profession!**

## CHAPTER VII

# The pH Power
# of Barley Leaves

In describing the outstanding qualities of barley leaves as a food with real power, the fact that it is highly alkaline is a great advantage for those eating a typical American "high acid-ash" diet. To understand this, you need to understand the symbol pH. What does pH mean and why is it important?

### UNDERSTANDING pH

The pH is the measurement of the ratio between acids and alkalines in our body fluids — ranging from 0 to 14.0 with neutral being 7.0. Acid is from 0 to 7.0 and alkaline 7.0 to 14.0.

A list of the pH of some of the most important substances would include the following:[1]

| | | |
|---|---|---|
| **Acid:** | Stomach Acid (HCl)........1.0 | Urine ...........................6.0 |
| | Gastric Acid.....................1.4 | |
| **Neutral:** | Pure Water ......................7.0 | |
| **Alkaline:** | Blood................................7.35 | Bile...............................7.5 |
| | Pancreatic Juice .............8.5 | |

A quick way to determine a person's pH balance is to check the pH of his urine. From the above list, you can see that if a person's urine pH, for example, is on the acid side, the pH is expressed as a lower number on the pH scale than if it is normal. The opposite is true of alkaline urine. It would be expressed by a number higher than average and the doctor would say you have a higher than normal pH. One of the keys to vibrant health, therefore, is keeping your pH in balance.

## BALANCED pH — A KEY TO GOOD HEALTH

A high urine pH usually indicates the person is not drinking enough water. Few Americans, I am told, drink adequate amounts of water — not **liquids** — but water for good health. Our gallons of soft drinks, iced tea and instant beverage mixes don't count. Your weight in pounds divided by two is the correct number of ounces of water needed daily. **If you're suffering from poor and/or slow digestion, low energy and a sluggish colon, your problem may be easily corrected by drinking more water!**

The key to vibrant health is partly a matter of keeping your pH in balance. The cells in our body cannot function if the pH varies too far from the narrow range of 7.35 to 7.45. The maintenance of a constant pH ultimately depends upon the excretory action of the lungs and the kidneys. (The three major mechanisms for controlling acid-base equilibrium are complex and require some knowledge of chemistry to be understood. I am assuming that most readers would rather understand the influence of diet rather than body chemistry on the acid-base balance.)

## ACID-BASE FORMING FOODS

After foods we eat are digested, they break down into either acid or an alkaline end-product in our tissues. This end-product is called the "ash," and remains in the body. Foods which produce an alkaline ash are "base-forming" foods, and those producing acid ash are called "acid-forming." These terms refer to the way the body uses our foods; it has nothing to do with the way they taste in your mouth. This is an important concept for you to remember.

Most people misunderstand this principle. Here is a common illustration. A number of popular fruits, such as oranges, lemons, limes, cherries, grapefruit, etc., are sour and taste acid. Upon ingestion, however, they break down into a base-forming (alkaline) ash. This is a fact, but the average person, not understanding it, typically responds, "I don't care what anybody says, grapefruit is too acid for my system and I won't touch it."

Only prunes, plums, rhubarb or cranberries burn leaving an acid ash and can accurately be claimed for making body fluids acid! If citrus fruit, for example, causes acidosis symptoms, it is because the citric acid has stirred up acid products already in the body, for the purpose of detoxifying and eliminating them. This reaction may be uncomfortable, but is beneficial. If it happens to you, cut back on citrus for a few days and then resume eating small quantities occasionally until the problem passes.[2]

The body needs both types of foods. It is better, however, when alkaline (base-forming) foods slightly predominate over acid-forming ones. The body can handle a wide range of acid-base foods without upsetting the balance. Today's American diet, however, has pushed above this range of normalcy. We have become too full of acid and, as a result, are experiencing a wide range of diseases that flourish in an acid medium. That is one reason why dried barley juice is such an outstanding food — it is highly alkaline.

When you understand the foods that are in each of these two categories, it becomes very clear why we are too acid in pH. Acid-forming foods are: meat, fish, poultry, eggs, cereal products, corn and sugars of all kinds. Alkaline-forming foods are: milk, nuts, fruits, vegetables and most seeds.[3] Can you see why our American diet needs changing? Indeed, it must be changed if we want to live a healthy and disease-free life.

## CARBOHYDRATE SOURCES

Let's consider carbohydrate foods and their contribution to the pH balance in our bodies . Carbohydrates are of two major types — sugars and starches. Both of these groups leave an acid-ash upon digestion. A list of some of the major foods in each category is given below:

| SUGARS | | STARCHES | |
|---|---|---|---|
| cane sugar | jellies | flours | cereals |
| beet sugar | jams | rice | whole grains |
| fruit juices | preserves | dried beans | sweet potatoes |
| soft drinks | dried fruits | dried peas | pasta |
| candy | levulose | | breads |
| cake icing | fructose | | |
| honey | maltose | | |
| molasses | lactose | | |
| syrups | glucose | | |
| | galactose | | |

When you add a few fresh foods to the above list, you have the major components of the meals of millions of Americans. Our intake of calories is very high, but our intake of nutrients is inadequate for vibrant health. That's why, in my estimation, the addition of dried barley leaves to our diet is such a simple, easy, quick way to supply the missing nutrients at an affordable price!

## CARBOHYDRATE BALANCE IS IMPERATIVE

It should be emphasized that about 80 percent of the carbohydrates you eat should be from the **starch** group and only 20 percent from the simple sugars. Since starch is a complex carbohydrate, it takes a much longer time to digest than sugar. Also, only 2 calories per minute go into the bloodstream from starch digestion while 10 calories per minute are released by the digestion of sugar. This is why the organs, tissues, nerves and other body parts react so violently to the "flood" received when we eat a high sugar-content food or a pure carbohydrate food. Our bodies were not designed by their Creator to handle such excessive amounts of simple sugars.

I feel sure that in reality our diets in this regard are reversed. We are eating 80 percent of our carbohydrates in the form of sugar and 20 percent in the form of starch. Even with this in mind, it is only too easy to overdo on sugar consumption while eating what you think is starch. A hamburger bun from McDonald's, for instance, might not taste sweet to you, but sugar is a major ingredient in many starch products.

Many doctors with some nutrition training would give assent to a whole list of diseases caused or aggravated by our high sugar intake. Clearly, that list would include obesity, arteriosclerosis, heart disease, cancer, diabetes, arthritis, kidney stones, dental problems, high blood pressure, hyperactivity, hypoglycemia and many others.

## FIBER AND WATER HELP MAINTAIN pH BALANCE

We hear a lot about fiber these days. Cellulose (plant fiber) is also a carbohydrate. The body's ability to digest cellulose is very poor, but it gives bulk and helps with the elimination of waste from the intestinal tract. A friend of mine who is a medical doctor said in a lecture that 90 percent of bowel cancer could be eliminated by eating 2-3 tablespoons of bran and drinking 6-8 glasses of water daily. Foods high in cellulose are: bran, dried fruits, legumes, fruits with skins, seedy fruits, green leafy vegetables (kale, collards, mustard greens, turnip greens, kohlrabi, etc.) and coarse fiber vegetables such as celery.[4]

Dr. Dennis Burkett, a surgeon who spent many years in South Africa, has written books and articles stating that in societies where the diet is composed of 80 percent complex carbohydrates (meaning starches), the people are healthy, robust, and free of many of our medical problems. Vegetarians are healthier; all kinds of research studies prove that point.

The body has a great backup system for making fantastic chemical adjustments quickly when we do foolish things such as drinking a quart of freshly squeezed orange juice (alkaline) at one sitting or eating a 16-oz. steak (acid) with lots of french fries (acid) and soda pop (acid) for dinner. Nonetheless, we all know how common it is to see our family and friends taking some kind of antacid tablet after eating. It is so common that we consider it "natural" — like cavities in our teeth! We need to reconsider our attitudes about these abnormal conditions and to be more careful in planning our meals.[5]

You may find it interesting to compare qualities of certain foods in their ability to leave an acid or base residue in the body. (See Table 4.) Generally, one may eat freely of the base-forming foods and sparingly of acid-forming foods.

## ACIDOSIS AND ALKALOSIS

Many more people suffer from acidosis than alkalosis, and diet is only one factor involved here. A list of the four most common causes of acidosis, other than food intake, would include: **Diarrhea** — one of the most frequent causes. Among children, it is one of the most common causes of death; **Diabetes Mellitus** — diabetics cannot properly metabolize glucose and this causes a rapid rise in acid production; **Kidney Disease** — malfunctioning kidneys result in the third major cause of acidosis; **Vomiting** — may cause a loss of both acid and alkali and result in metabolic acidosis.

Acidosis can also be caused by liver problems, shock, excess intake of salt, meat, fatty foods, obesity, fever, a too-rapid heartbeat, malnutrition, stress and many other things.

The major effect of acidosis is depression of the central nervous system. People first become depressed, then disoriented and later can go into a coma, if they are not properly treated.

The most common symptoms of an imbalanced pH is heartburn. A burning sensation in the pit of the stomach and burping of a highly acid liquid are sure symptoms of acidosis. Along with these, complaints of bloating, belching and a "full feeling" after a small amount of food are commonly reported.

## TABLE 4

### Relative Acid & Base Forming Quality[6]

(100-calorie portions)

| Food | Acid Ash (mg.) | Food | Alkaline Ash (mg.) |
|------|----------------|------|---------------------|
| Oysters | 30.0 | Spinach | 113.0 |
| Haddock | 12.0 | Cucumber | 45.5 |
| Smelt | 10.1 | Celery | 42.5 |
| Chicken | 10.0 | Chard, Swiss | 41.1 |
| Egg, white | 9.5 | Lettuce | 38.6 |
| Halibut | 7.8 | Figs, dried | 32.3 |
| Whitefish | 7.6 | Tomato, fresh | 24.5 |
| Egg, whole | 7.5 | Carrots | 24.0 |
| Egg, yolk | 7.0 | Olives | 18.8 |
| Beef, round, lean | 6.7 | Parsnips | 18.2 |
| Mackerel, fresh | 6.7 | Cabbage | 18.0 |
| Veal, breast, lean | 6.7 | Cauliflower | 17.4 |
| Salmon | 5.4 | Pineapple, fresh | 15.7 |
| Turkey | 3.7 | Orange juice | 14.4 |
| Cracked wheat | 3.3 | Lemons | 12.0 |
| Shredded wheat | 3.3 | Apricots, fresh | 11.0 |
| Lamb, breast of | 3.3 | Radishes | 9.8 |
| Oatmeal | 3.0 | Potatoes | 8.6 |
| Barley, pearl | 2.9 | Raisins | 6.8 |
| Bread, whole wheat | 2.7 | Squash | 6.1 |
| Bread, white | 2.7 | Buttermilk | 6.1 |
| Rice | 2.7 | Apple, fresh | 6.0 |
| Mutton, chuck | 2.0 | Pear, fresh | 5.6 |
| Peas, green | 1.2 | Milk, whole | 2.6 |

## ACIDOSIS SYMPTOMS

There are a number of other symptoms one can observe that also indicate the presence of an acid excess. Here is a partial list: breathlessness, frequent sighing, irregular breathing, "cold sweat" perspiration, dryness of skin or mouth or throat, insomnia, hyperirritability, diminished urination, dry-hard stool, tachycardia (fast heartbeat), intolerance of light, restlessness, canker sores, easily broken or weak and peeling fingernails.[7]

So, what treatment should you consider if you have an acid stomach? One thing that you should not do is take products that contain sodium bicarbonate and other alkalinizing salts. Continued use of these easily-available, over-the-counter antacids may induce alkalosis, which causes your problems to become even more complex.

## THE PARADOX OF ANTACID USE

Before you begin to self-diagnose and self-medicate, however, I want you to hear an additional fact. Too little acid is a common problem among the general population. According to one doctor who uses pH titration for measuring stomach acidity (few doctors test for this, actually), 35-50 percent of those tested had too little stomach acid rather than too much. This is especially true in patients who have been taking antacids regularly. In that group, more than 50 percent had below normal levels of acidity.

For years Americans have been bombarded on TV with extremely clever ads leaving the impression that almost everyone needs an aid for faulty digestion. In 1982 the sale of over-the-counter antacid preparations is reported to have totaled more than one-half billion dollars, so we have believed these Madison Avenue experts.

Our choices of products are in the hundreds. They come in liquid, tablet, capsule, and fizzing powder — all for the single purpose of neutralizing stomach acid. Taking these products, however, does not in any way deal with the cause of too much acid, if indeed one exists. It simply masks the symptoms and makes your overall health worse if you are a habitual user over a long period of time.

If you are already a regular user of antacid products, on what basis did you make your choice of brand to be used? The ads we see on TV are not a scientifically sound basis for choosing between the more than 100 products available. Why? Because they tell the facts about tests in vitro (in a glass container), not in vivo (within the human body). Only what happens inside of us really matters!

## SIDE EFFECTS OF VARIOUS ANTACID COMPOUNDS

So, if you are an antacid user, do you know the major ingredient of your antacid? Is there more than one active ingredient? Do you realize the dangers of masking symptoms which warn of the presence of serious illness?

The oldest and perhaps most common antacid is sodium bicarbonate, which is ordinary baking soda. It is extremely effective in neutralizing stomach acid, and it does its job rapidly. Sounds great, doesn't it? Problems, however, do exist with its use. Because of its efficiency in neutralizing acid, sodium bicarbonate can **seriously** upset the acid-base balance in the body, causing alkalosis.

It also contains very high amounts of sodium that anyone on a sodium-restricted diet or suffering from heart disease, kidney disease or high blood pressure should avoid. People with poor kidney function need to stay away from it because it can lead to recurrent urinary tract infections (from urine becoming alkaline) and kidney stone formation with prolonged use. In addition, several products, whose main ingredient is sodium bicarbonate, contain other ingredients, such as aspirin, which are actually harmful to an already irritated stomach lining! Be sure to check your labels before buying and taking these products.[8]

Calcium carbonate is probably the most effective antacid, and it has no effect on the acid-base balance. It often causes constipation, however, requiring laxatives. It is another principal antacid found in numerous over-the-counter products. It, like sodium bicarbonate, works fast and is quite effective.

With prolonged or excessive use, calcium carbonate is capable of causing kidney malfunction and stone formation, as well as high blood calcium levels. If that's not bad enough, one study published in a prestigious medical journal reported that ingestion of calcium carbonate creates an "acid rebound" effect that is, after temporarily neutralizing excess acid, it causes the body to produce even more acid as a result![9]

A third major antacid ingredient is magnesium, in one of several compounds. These compounds are generally safe (except for those with chronic disease) but they have a laxative effect many people cannot tolerate.[10]

A fourth giant on the list of antacids is the compound aluminum hydroxide. Although its action is good over a prolonged time, it is slow to begin to work and can cause severe constipation. Until recently, researchers believed that the body eliminated the aluminum present in medications. New findings indicate that some of it is absorbed into the bloodstream, and from there it can accumulate in other target areas, most notably the brain.[11]

This news is alarming, especially in light of the fact that the accumulation of aluminum in brain cells has been associated with Alzheimer's disease. Many of the best-selling antacids combine aluminum and magnesium compounds, causing the American's average daily consumption of aluminum to rise from 20 mgs. to 100 mgs. or more. Is the aluminum "load" from antacids poisoning us?

Always remember, no matter what type of antacid you use, check with your doctor. Acid indigestion, "sour stomach" and "heartburn" are signs that the body is having problems. Don't mistake heartburn for a heart attack.

The latest series of TV ads that I have seen promoting antacids tout these products as an effective source of calcium. We know, don't we, that nearly all Americans need more calcium? We have epidemic proportions of osteoporosis, weak backs, loose teeth, brittle fingernails and many other conditions related to insufficient calcium supplies. But, which company tells us that the calcium in antacids is nonusable, for the most part, because it does not contain the nutrients required for synergistic action with the calcium! None of them do, of course! Barley leaves, not antacids, are an almost ideal product for this purpose. They are a rich natural source of calcium and have generous amounts of all the minerals required for its use.

Before leaving the subject of acidosis, one more topic should be mentioned. Much has been written about the adverse effect of stress on one's acid-base balance. Mental, physical, emotional and financial stress all produce an acid overload.

There is no doubt that worry, fear, anxiety, jealousy, hatred, bitterness, anger, unforgiveness and phobias of all kinds play havoc with the acid-base balance and our state of health.

One physician stated it so well when he said something like this: There are no medications available that can be dispensed to deal with the acids that are produced by negative thoughts, attitudes and emotions. These things require spiritual, not physical, healing. (I believe this as well!)

## SYMPTOMS OF ALKALOSIS

What about alkalosis — what are the symptoms, causes and treatments for this condition? The symptoms, actually, are often similar to those for acidosis. Determining which you have is sometimes difficult and requires the help of a professional. Some common symptoms of excess alkali are: chronic indigestion, tiredness after eating a meal, heavy and slow pulse, night cramps, stiffness in joints, "thick" blood, high cholesterol, stone formation, osteoarthritis, asthma, "crawling sensation" of the skin, night coughs.[12]

As with acidosis, there are many possible causes of alkalosis. Some common ones are: diarrhea, vomiting, excess carbohydrate intake, stress, kidney disease, bronchitis, inflamed prostate, menopausal disorders, general endocrine imbalance and others.

## CHECKING YOUR OWN pH BALANCE

Two methods recommended for determining if your indigestion is due to an acid or alkaline imbalance are as follows:

- Drink four sips of an apple cider or wine vinegar mixture made from the following recipe: 2 tablespoons of vinegar in 1 cup of cool water. If you receive relief, you have alkalosis; if your heartburn is aggravated, you have acidosis.
- Place pH paper or litmus paper in the saliva of the mouth. Red litmus turns blue in an alkali media. Blue litmus turns red in an acid media.[13]

### A pH BALANCED DIET

Balancing the diet with acid foods, taking extra vitamin C (which is acid) and a digestive pill containing hydrochloric acid will relieve alkalosis. Alkali-forming minerals are sodium, potassium, calcium and magnesium. Foods containing these minerals would be helpful in restoring a pH balance.

In summary, the typical American diet tends to produce "acid stomachs." TV ads have certainly taught us that! This is true because we are eating excessive amounts of foods such as meats, fish, poultry, sugar, soda pop, eggs, cheese, legumes and cereals that burn and leave an acid ash. We eat much smaller amounts of alkaline-forming foods which include vegetables, fruits, (except plums, prunes, rhubarb and cranberries) milk and most nuts.

### A TRUE STORY

A true story will bring me to the final point of this whole chapter. One day my late husband and I were eating lunch at a cafeteria where three women sat at the table next to us. It was apparent these women were sisters lookalikes in facial features as well as in their "heavyset" body types.

One of them reached in her purse and brought out a pint-sized bottle of Tums. (Frankly, I didn't know Tums could be purchased in such a large container.) She said, "Well, I might as well get out my Tums, for I know I will need to take them when I'm finished eating. I can't eat **anything** anymore without having indigestion."

Another sister said, "You, too? I'm that way myself. It's just gotten to the place that I can hardly enjoy eating for dreading the way I feel afterwards."

Believe it or not, sister No. 3 added her story with somewhat the same words sister No. 2 had just expressed.

I said to my husband, "Would you care if I went to their table to tell them about dried barley juice?" He quickly replied, "No, please don't do that. You can't save the whole world, so just relax and enjoy your lunch."

When they finished eating, two sisters left for the restroom and that was my chance. I popped up from my table and went over to the sister who remained seated. I apologized for interrupting, and then told her about the high alkalinity of green barley leaves and how I believed it would be so much better for them to take than any drug-store concoction.

A few days later, they each bought a jar and two weeks later, one of the sisters phoned to say that not only had their belching and burping and gas problems stopped, but all of them were experiencing much more energy and a general feeling of well-being.

The bottom line is this: Dried barley juice is an excellent source of alkalinity to counter our acid-ash diet. This makes it truly a food with real power.

## MARCH, 1998

There is a new "Model for Health" that I believe offers hope to millions of us who want an alternative to America's traditional medical model.

The philosophical basis acknowledges first that the body was created, not evolved by accident. Health, therefore, can only be achieved by gaining understanding of how the body was designed to function.

Designing strategies for assisting the body's natural mechanisms for health and healing has been the passion for years of Sam Queen and his associates.* They have been researching for procedures and products that result in optimal health, with longevity.

This Health Model proposes that the body's breakdown can be charted by observing five subclinical defects that lead to disease, along with accompanying symptoms. Following is their list, with a few representative symptoms or diseases in each defect.

## 1. Acidemia  (acid pH)
Tooth decay; GI problems; chronic fatigue; stones; infections; asthma; allergies; hardening of arteries; and the start of all degenerative disease; etc.

**2. Free Calcium Excess**
Arthritis; pseudo-gout; hypertension; calculus on teeth; malignancies; cancer; angina; poor vision; etc.

**3. Chronic Inflammation**
Autoimmune diseases (lupus, MS, diabetes, rheumatoid arthritis); etc.

**4. Connective Tissue Breakdown**
Loosened teeth; varicose veins; hernia; aneurysm; hemorrhoids; hiatal hernia; sagging skin; etc.

**5. Oxidative Stress**
Aging; dry skin; Parkinson's: Alzheimer's; Type II Diabetes; brain and nerve disorders; etc.

The manufacturer provided perfect instructions for prevention and cure of disease in His manual! **We are fools for ignoring or rejecting His plan.**


\* Queen and Company, PO Box 49308, Colorado Springs, Co., 80949-9308. Phone (719) 598-4968

## CHAPTER VIII

# The Nutritional Significance of Enzymes

A unique and outstanding characteristic of barley leaves is the hundreds of "live" enzymes they contain. Several of these have been isolated and studied for their healing properties.

Why is this such significant information? I will try to answer simply; but, first, I want to help you develop a healthy respect for the body's need for and use of enzymes.

## WHAT ARE ENZYMES?

In nutrition, **enzymes are chemical substances required by every living cell for every biochemical process**. In breathing, for example, enzymes are involved in the exchange of oxygen and carbon dioxide in the lungs. They determine our responses to temperature changes. They are needed for reactions like muscle contraction, nerve conduction, urine excretion, and for almost everything else! They actually fix not only the length of our lifespan but how effectively we maintain a high state of health and freedom from disease. It behooves us to learn that enzymes are precious commodities worth understanding and protecting.

## ENZYMES IN DIGESTION AND ASSIMILATION

The major goal in this chapter is to discuss food enzymes in the context of digestion and assimilation — the distribution of nutrients to individual cells. If we lack enzymes needed for digestion, it might take us years to digest our supper. It is probably important for you to know there is a great deal of new knowledge about food enzymes.

Scientists had been telling us for years that enzymes are catalysts — substances which can spark a reaction within a cell. It was said that they may either speed up, slow down, or interfere with processes, but that they themselves were not altered by what occurred. It was believed that they were used and reused without being destroyed. Because of new research in the field, many scientists have abandoned those ideas.

## ENZYMES HAVE LIFE FORCE

It is now theorized that enzymes work on both a chemical and biological level and that **every enzyme has a life force — a vitality at its very core** — that is the body's labor force in maintaining health and healing. Scientists know there is a life principle, but they cannot assemble it in a test tube to be measured or studied. They do know, however, that it is there.[1]

Students of enzymology say that were it not for this life principle, humans would be no more than a heap of lifeless materials, a pile of dirt. Chemical substances of which we are made — proteins, vitamins, minerals, and water — are lifeless and useless, they say, until acted upon in metabolism by the enzymes.[2] If this is true, can you see how important it is for us to understand them?

This new theory also states that every person has a given, limited amount of enzyme energy at birth; it must last for the person's lifetime. According to this theory, **when we use up our enzyme supply quickly, such as by eating all cooked or processed foods that have no enzymes, our lives are shortened.**[3] In addition to destroying enzymes by cooking, we also increase the need for them by eating "junk foods," drinking alcohol, smoking cigarettes, taking drugs, eating pork, shrimp, lobster, clams, catfish, etc., and by breathing impure air and drinking impure water, to name a few.

## DEPLETED ENZYMES LINKED TO ILLNESS

**Depleting our enzyme supply results in a weakened immune system.** Weakening our immune system results in making us prime targets for cancer, heart disease, arthritis, diabetes, obesity, AIDS, allergies, and many other degenerative diseases. As several researchers have pointed out, millions of Americans experience death at middle-age instead of living out their full allotment of 70 years.

Dr. Edward Howell explains this modern problem this way:

*"With heavy withdrawals of enzymes needed to digest an almost all-cooked diet, it's not hard to see how we would become metabolically enzyme-poor even in middle-age. Heavy withdrawals and skimpy deposits of enzymes lead to eventual bankruptcy.*

*Unfortunately, the glands and the major organs, including the brain, suffer most from the unnatural digestive drain on the metabolic enzyme potential."*[4]

Dr. Howell suggests **we substitute raw calories for cooked ones as much as possible,** using such foods as raw milk, bananas, avocados, seeds, nuts, grapes, and many other natural foods which are moderately high both in calories and food enzymes.

The digestion of a raw-food meal takes more time, but does not use up as many of the endogenous (made inside the body) digestive enzyme secretions (pancreatic juice, pepsin, erypsin, amylase, ptyalin, etc.) as does digestion of a cooked-food meal. This relieves the digestive burden of the organs and glands. It is also a way of sparing the life principle in enzymes so that, theoretically at least, the person lives a longer life, has better health, and has more enzyme potential for healing.[5]

In summary, it can be said: enzymes are protein carriers charged with vital energy factors, but like the battery in your flashlight, the energy is exhaustible and we must learn to conserve it.

## ENZYMES AND WEIGHT CONTROL

Another idea that may be new to most readers is the connection some enzymologists believe exists between enzymes and weight control. Dr. Edward Howell explains this in his book, *Enzyme Nutrition.* Here is a review of his theory.

Dr. Howell believes research shows conclusively that certain foods stimulate glands and cause them to be overactive.

Two glands known especially to be involved in this are the pituitary gland (which is the body's secretion control center) and the pancreas (which secretes digestive enzymes for all three major types of food: protein, fat, and carbohydrates). **Research shows that cooked foods excite these glands and tend to be fattening, while raw foods tend to be relatively nonstimulating and result in stabilized weights.**[6]

This principle was shown in an experiment where the goal was to fatten hogs for market quickly and economically. Feeding hogs cooked potatoes produced the desired results even after the heavy cost of labor, etc., for the cooking of the potatoes.[7]

A study which confirmed these results was done on humans who were fed lots of fresh fruits (i.e., bananas, avocados, apples, oranges, etc.), and milk. The calorie intake was rather high, but the participants did not gain weight. The conclusion: cooked foods result in the production of more fat.[8]

Enzymes also seem to affect weight in other circumstances. Studies done in Germany and at the University of Illinois show rats had lower body weight and higher enzyme activity in the pancreas and fat cells when they ate only once a day.[9]

While I have not personally participated in research of this nature, I have observed a number of persons who ate only one or two meals per day and have seen that they never had a weight problem. A few, in fact, seem to be below the ideal weight for their age, sex, body build, and occupation but have a great deal of energy for sustained labor. These persons are, incidentally, adhering primarily to a vegetarian diet which could be assumed to be higher in exogenous (made outside the body) enzymes.

## PATHOLOGY CONFIRMS VITAL ROLE OF ENZYMES

Pathologists have contributed to the formulation of this new theory. They know that when autopsies are performed, enzyme content of the pancreas widely differs. **Those who died from cancer, diabetes, liver problems, and other debilitating diseases have markedly fewer enzymes in their pancreas than persons who were healthy when they died.**[10]

Sick cells, especially cancer cells, rob the body of nutrients and prevent the production of enzymes. Thus, cancer cadavers, upon analysis, show a reduced enzyme level in their bodies. This having been laboratory proven, how can we help conserve our enzyme supply? **We must learn to eat daily a good supply of raw foods.** All raw foods contain enzymes. No cooked foods have any enzymes left in them — none at all!

## LIVE FOOD: LIVE ENZYMES
## DEAD FOOD: DEAD ENZYMES

During research on dehydrated green beans for my Master's Degree, I learned about that. Blanching (scalding) bite-size pieces of green beans for more than one minute resulted in total enzyme loss. Heat destruction of enzymes begins at 107°F. and is complete at 122°F. **So, no enzyme survives boiling** (212°F.), and even enzymes in milk pasteurized at 145°F. are destroyed. We must eat raw foods. More on this later.

The 20th century American diet with all of its man-made, high-tech, "dead" foods has created a critical shortage of enzymes. Do you realize that most, if not all, **boxed products have been subjected to a number of processes involving high temperatures until they are enzymeless?** So, the more your breakfasts and other meals are made of pre-prepared foods (in boxes, cans, or frozen), the more deficient you are in exogenous enzymes.

Another illustration of how a nearly perfect food has been made harmful to consumers, is the way we have completely changed the chemical nature of milk. **More than 90 percent of the enzymes in milk are destroyed by modern-day pasteurization methods.** Chemists have identified 35 separate enzymes in raw milk, with lipase (the fat digesting enzyme) one of the chief factors. Undoubtedly, the high incidence of clogged arteries of Americans is partly due to our high intake of homogenized milk — pasteurized milk with too few enzymes to make it digestible.[11]

Unpasteurized milk and butter were used for thousands of years without conferring degenerative disease on their users. Why was that? Because the milk and butter were raw, and anything which nature made for man's consumption as food contains the proper chemical substances in it to make it life-giving to the body. People lived for thousands of years without any atherosclerosis, heart disease, obesity, and other degenerative diseases that we suffer now in epidemic proportions.

**A fourth illustration of turning good food into bad is our conversion of oil into margarine.** Oils, in their natural state, are unsaturated fats which our bodies were designed to digest perfectly. The addition of hydrogen to those oils to make them into margarine and shortening creates a plastic-like material which the body has no digestive pathway for handling. All it can do is lay this material down in the arteries, thus creating circulation problems, hardening of the arteries, and eventual heart disease. One physician I heard lecturing to other physicians said he believes **margarine is the single most dangerous food on the American market!**

Illustrations of this type could fill another book by itself. It all boils down to the fact that man has tampered with nature's perfect plan in the realm of foods and nutrition and turned it into a money-making operation that ignores the ill effects such processing has on the consumer. We are dying like flies from what the agribusiness and commercial food giants have done to the food supply!

## *OLD TESTAMENT FOOD LAWS: SCIENTIFICALLY UP-TO-DATE*

Another very, very important way we can conserve our inherited supply of enzymes would be to follow the rules God gave the Israelites as recorded in the Bible. It is interesting to note that much of the "new" wisdom on these subjects corroborates the ideas behind dietary laws practiced by the Hebrews way back in 6,000 B.C. I have found it fascinating to study what the prophet Moses told the people regarding the types and preparation of food they could (and could not) eat. You can find the detailed list of this information in the Old Testament books of Leviticus (Chapter 11) and Deuteronomy (Chapter 14). I have chosen just a few examples upon which to enlarge.

One of the most outstanding examples would be the command, "Eat no pig" (TLB). You don't need to be reminded that pork in its many forms (bacon, ham, sausage, BBQ) is an all-American favorite. We love the taste of smoked, cured pork, and we eat it in very large quantities. Are we doing the right thing? Absolutely NOT — unless our goal is to exhaust our enzyme supply, rob ourselves of good health, and shorten our lives with degenerative diseases.

Don't you find it curious that the Hebrews of Bible times — back when people were supposed to be naive, ignorant, and superstitious — had better habits than we do when it came to eating. Let me explain the seriousness of our pork-eating patterns.

Recently, my pastor visited a dying friend in a cancer treatment center off the coast of the United States. The night he was there, a German doctor spoke to the patients and their families. His whole lecture was on enzymes and the need for us to conserve the internal life forces which we were given at birth. He made the statement that because the pig is the "earth's garbage can," **the consumption of pork requires thousands of enzymes to detoxify the flesh before the stomach can digest it.** In the stomach and small intestine, it requires additional hundreds of enzymes to digest and assimilate it. Because Americans are short on enzymes, this doctor said that we are not adequately digesting the pork. It lies in our intestines, putrefies, forms carcinogens, and we show up with cancer. His advice was for us not to eat pork at all.

A humorous situation occurred when my pastor spoke to him after his lecture and said, "Leviticus said for us not to eat pork, and we have ignored that advice." The doctor replied, "I have never heard of Dr. Leviticus nor read his published works, but I know from my own research that the eating of pork is a major cause of cancer and other degenerative diseases."

At this point, I would like to ask you a question. Did you really hear what has been said about eating pork? Do you want to live a long, healthy, disease-free life? Then, as much as possible, eliminate pork from your diet.

Have I finished taking away your gastronomical pleasure? No! For the very same reason you should eliminate shrimp, catfish, lobster, oysters, and clams from your diet also, because they are the "garbage cans" of the rivers and oceans. Consuming them is extremely destructive to the limited supply of our enzymes. If we will make these sacrifices of eating pleasure, we will live longer, healthier, and more productive lives, while we greatly reduce our risk of dying from some of our worst killer diseases. Think about it!

## ENZYMES: KEY TO LONGEVITY?

Yes, enzymes are a key to longevity. As we grow older, there seems to be diminished secretion of enzymes in the stomach and intestinal tract. This results in poor digestion and assimilation and a malnourished condition that results in a weakened body with less vitality. Death overtakes those with depleted enzymes more quickly than those whose enzymes remain strong enough to digest and assimilate their food.

It is only recently that this information is being used in the medical diagnostic processes and as a viable therapeutic tool. It is now possible to test the enzymes in urine and determine, with a great deal of accuracy, their shortages and excesses. Several cancer centers off the shores of the United States are successfully using enzymology as a treatment modality for this killer disease. Perhaps this is one of the reasons why their cure rate is so superior to the American standard procedure! **An international study has now proven that chemotherapy, radiation, drugs, and surgery are not the answers to cancer!**

In my limited experience, I have found that doctors from several other countries, especially Germany, have latched on to the use of enzymes as a viable treatment modality for the aged as well as for the diseased. It is reported that Dr. Hans Nieper of Hanover, West Germany, has a 74 percent cancer cure rate compared to 17 percent in the United States.

## ENZYMES IN THE TREATMENT OF CANCER

In his treatment of cancer patients, Dr. Nieper uses enzyme therapy in addition to a strict vegetarian diet, with the use of almost no drugs and absolutely no chemotherapy or radiation. Wouldn't it be wonderful if American doctors would at least give us a choice in treatment modalities for degenerative diseases? This is true especially regarding the "Big Four" — heart disease, cancer, diabetes, and atherosclerosis.

## VITAMINS ARE COENZYMES

Digestive enzymes do not work alone; they have quite a host of helpers called co-enzymes. Vitamins are in this category. That being true, it is also easy to see the importance of getting enough (but not too much) of the vitamins required for optimal enzymatic function. Do we need to supplement our diet with vitamin pills? It will be wonderful when scientists can accurately assess the status of the body's vitamin levels. Until then, I believe modest supplementation IS a good idea.

From our chemically treated soil, to our chemically processed foods, packed in chemically treated packages, it is anybody's guess what the vitamin and mineral content of today's foods actually is. Three examples of recent reports explain this: A few months ago, a new crop of cabbage was tested for its vitamin C value. Since cabbage is a food rich in vitamin C, the farmer was shocked to find that the amount of vitamin C in his sample was too small to register on the equipment being used by the government agency. Can you imagine that? Unfortunately, this is by no means an isolated case.

A few weeks later, I was talking with a Pennsylvania farmer who for years has grown carrots for the commercial market. His mature crop has always been tested using a Refractometer to gauge the carrots mineral level. The measurement scale ranges from 1 to 22 with the latter being the highest possible score.

For many years his carrot crop measured around 16, a very acceptable score. In recent years, as modern farming methods replaced organic farming, his carrots have measured 4 to 6! Unfortunately, we consumers are the ones who are registering, if not suffering, the loss. The farmer's profit on his crops has probably remained fairly constant, if not increased a bit.

In 1985, Fairleigh Dickinson University duplicated an older study of protein content of wheat grown on a particular field of their farm. They found it had dropped from 17 percent in 1945 to nine percent in 1985. That opens a whole can of worms about our farming methods which I will resist writing about at this time.

## FRESH, RAW FOODS TO THE RESCUE

Can you see, now, why we must eat fresh, raw foods every day? Do you understand why our **American diets are so devoid of "live" enzymes?** Literally, remember this: no enzymes, no digestion; no enzymes, no assimilation; no digestion or assimilation, no vibrant health; and certainly no resistance to killer diseases. Therefore, the wise man will see to it that all of his food intake in a day's time is not "dead" from the point of view of enzymes. Raw fruits and vegetables truly are a significant requirement to a healthy diet. And remember, dried barley juice is a raw food, and it contains hundreds of "live" enzymes. (At this writing, approximately 300 enzymes have been isolated. Dr. Hagiwara is quoted as saying he suspects there may be as many as 1,000 enzymes in the green leaves of barley.)

## TYPES OF ENZYMES:
### ENDOGENOUS & EXOGENOUS

Until now, we have only talked about enzymes found in raw foods. Nature has placed within each food on this planet both plant and animal — specific enzymes needed for at least the beginning stages of its digestion. Intensive study of this subject should humble the greatest of scholars! No person or committee could ever have conceived such a perfect plan for giving mankind everything we need for cell LIFE. Enzymes in the green leaves of barley are such an outstanding example of this that special attention is paid to it in the next chapter.

Enzymes are not only found in raw, unprocessed food, but **two types are also produced inside the body**. These digestive enzymes are synthesized by the glands and organs of the digestive tract. Table 5 gives you a bird's-eye view of this second category of enzymes. For a more detailed study, consult almost any college textbook on nutrition.

**TABLE 5**

**DIGESTIVE ENZYMES
AND SOURCES OF THEIR PRODUCTION**

| Source | Digestion of Starches | Digestion of Fat | Digestion of Protein |
|---|---|---|---|
| Mouth | Ptyalin in Saliva | None | None |
| Stomach | None | None | Pepsin Hydrochloric acid |
| Pancreas | Amylase | Lipase | Trypsin Chymotrypsin |
| Small Intestine | Amylase Maltase Lactase Sucrase Lipase | Enteric Lipase | Carboxy-polypeptidase |

The third enzyme category is metabolic enzymes products of the endocrine glands (thyroid, parathyroid, adrenal, and pituitary). These enzymes build, repair, and maintain the functioning of every organ, tissue and cell. They actually build the body from proteins, carbohydrates and fats. Without them, life is impossible. In fact, old age and worn-out metabolic enzyme activity are always twin concepts. You don't see one without the other. This is also true in the lives of mammals other than man.

Following digestion in the mouth, in the stomach, and in the small intestine, food must be assimilated (absorbed by our 78 to 83 trillion cells) before it gives life to the body. Thus, **we are not what we eat as much as we are what we digest and metabolize because of the quantity and quality of enzymes in our system.**

## DID YOU KNOW YOUR DIGESTIVE SYSTEM TALKS TO YOU?

We must pay attention to what our digestive system says to us, especially today! A typical American diet is overheated, overcooked, and overprocessed, which makes it enzyme-deficient. This means the pancreas, salivary glands, and other organs are unable to carry through on their natural responsibilities. As a result, we experience belching, burning in the stomach, gas in the intestines and many other unpleasantly familiar symptoms.

## ENZYMES ARE INDISPENSABLE

Here is the bottom line: Enzyme action is required at every step in these complex processes. Our quality of health is largely a result of enzymic action inside us. Our bodies build enzymes from amino acids (the components of protein — similar in chemical structure to egg white). Enzymes examined under a microscope are complex chains of amino acids. The specific arrangement of molecules in their chain determines their function.

Starches require amylases to aid in their digestion, and no other molecular structure will work. Proteins require proteases and fats require lipases. Understanding the absolute necessity of having each of these "cell firecrackers" can help you see the value of taking a teaspoon of dried barley leaves daily or of daily eating deep-green leafy vegetables and other fresh foods. Remember this; good enzymic action is necessary for life, and it is not possible to have good enzyme action when the necessary nutrients are lacking in your body. These nutrients will not be present for your use unless you eat a proper diet or take adequate supplements on a regular basis.

## GREEN BARLEY: BURSTING WITH "LIVE" ENZYMES

Authorities disagree on the total number of different enzymes or the total of all enzymes available for our use. One author said there were millions; others have said hundreds or tens-of-thousands. I am not sure which is correct. I feel, however, that **green leaves of the embryonic barley plant are an excellent source of hundreds of "live" enzymes.** This statement cannot be made for any man-made vitamin or mineral tablet. Most lack natural enzymes and, probably, enzymes from any source.

Barley leaves, in the raw state, are an excellent source of enzymes and co-enzymes (vitamins) required for the body's biochemical reactions. It is easy for me to believe they create the best possible atmosphere for healthy cell activity to flourish.

## DIGESTIVE ENZYME SUPPLEMENTS

Research has also produced evidence which suggests enzyme supplements should be used just as regularly and as faithfully as vitamin and mineral supplements. This is particularly true when people are older or suffering from a disease robbing them of the life-force needed to create enzymes. It is also true, enzyme supplements should be taken if we are not including generous quantities of raw foods in our daily food intake.

There is also plenty of research evidence to show eating simple meals instead of complex ones affects enzyme requirements. It has been shown conclusively that meals which contain many different kinds of food are difficult to digest. Each food requires its very own set of enzymes. Thus, a typical American salad bar meal, containing small amounts of many foods is a stress situation for the body! This is especially true when we complicate the problem with large quantities of oil containing salad dressing on top! Certainly there is plenty of research evidence to show high-calorie intake is also related to degenerative diseases such as obesity, heart disease and, especially cancer.

If you are having difficulty with digestion and decide you might like to try enzyme supplementation, there are a number of good products available at drugstores or health-food stores. When taken before meals, they work with dispatch more or less like those digestive enzymes made by the body. (See Appendix D for further suggestions.)

## A REVIEW OF IMPORTANT FACTS

Now let me review a few very important facts, before ending this chapter with the most important information of all about food with enzymic power.

- About 65 percent of food in our supermarkets has been processed (refined) and, thus, is enzymeless.
- No assimilation of nutrients is possible without enzymes.
- Enzymes must be "live" to be used by the body.
- Only fresh, raw, uncooked foods have "live" enzymes.
- No body building or repair of organs, tissues, or cells is possible without enzymes.
- Enzymes actually determine life span and quality of life.
- Diminished supply of enzymes means more potential for disease, especially degenerative diseases.
- Fast use of enzymes, such as in eating scavenger flesh from the air, land, or water, shortens life.
- Endogenous enzymes are limited at birth, are exhaustible, last longer when conserved by consistent daily consumption of raw foods, and by consuming supplements.

Now for the grand-finale message on enzymes as they relate to one single food with a worldwide reputation for dynamic enzymatic power the embryonic leaves of the barley plant. Barley leaves are the ideal, instant-food way for busy Americans to get their daily serving of raw, leafy greens. The next chapter will thoroughly cover the subject of enzymes in green barley leaves.

## CHAPTER IX

# Enzymatic Power in Young Barley Leaves

Now for the "good news" about the dynamic enzymatic power of fresh, raw, green barley leaves. According to Dr. Hagiwara, the juice from the young barley plants contains several hundred types of enzymes corresponding to those found in the human body cells. It is this multitude of enzymes, saved intact and "alive" by his method for making dried barley juice, which sets it absolutely in a class by itself.

### ENZYMES: "ON GUARD" AGAINST TOXINS

One of the very most important functions of enzymes is to neutralize poisons in the body. I want to mention a few of the specific enzymes in dried barley juice that can help purge the body of toxins which we absorb as pollutants in the air, water, and food we consume. Some of the enzymes that will resolve indigestible substances in our food, for example, are: phospholipase to resolve phospholipid, phosphatase to resolve glycophosphate, DNAase and RNAase to resolve nucleic acid, cytochrome oxidase, amine oxidase, alcohol dehydrogenase, and, most importantly, nitrate reductase, which is known to resolve all sorts of cancer-causing petroleum-base nitro-compounds.[1]

It is known that almost all chemical substances and environmental pollutants have carcinogenicity — the ability to produce cancers of many types. Seventy percent of carcinogens are nitric compounds, which are petroleum solvents. And, while it's particularly effective against them, nitrate reductase isn't the only component in barley juice which has been proven to act as an antidote to these poisonous nitro-compounds.[2]

Barley juice is particularly rich in two additional enzymes which can help nutritionally strengthen the body to resist and counteract mutations. Dr. Hagiwara and his research staff have isolated one barley juice molecule (a protoheme) with a molecular weight of 53,000. From this protoheme molecule, a sort of peroxidase can be extracted, which they have named $P_4D_1$. It definitely lessens the cancer-producing ability of the typical nitro-oxides and can also counteract toxic effects of BHT — a chemical used to preserve many food products.[3]

Of special importance is the fact that this peroxidase is more active in an acidic environment. Therefore, one would expect that barley leaves may possibly even begin decomposing cancer-producing substances in the stomach, where the digestive juices are highly acidic.[4]

Also, **$P_4D_1$ has been found to have an anti-peptic ulcer and anti-inflammatory function but with no side effects** as with ordinary anti-inflammatory drugs. It is thought to be superior to cortisone and non-steroid drugs (which have a common side effect of producing ulcers), such as phenylbutazone, widely used today as treatment for these problems.[5]

Most importantly, it was also reported at the 1981 Japan Pharmacy Science Association annual meeting that **$P_4D_1$ produces remarkable stimulation to DNA** (deoxy-ribonucleic acid the genetic chain) **repair, including even that in the reproductive cells.** Stimulation of DNA repair or promotion of reproductive cell activity has never been previously reported from the use of any natural OR synthetic source.[6]

It is widely known that many chemicals, including artificial food additives, can distort the human design genetically, resulting in birth defects. It is also clear **DNA breakage is involved in the development of some cancers.** Twenty years ago the FDA announced 3-4 benzpyrene from tobacco causes lung cancer. Since then, it has been discovered TRY-$P_1$ and TRY-$P_2$ tryptophanes in black char from broiled fish and charcoal-grilled meat are 20,000 times more carcinogenic than benzpyrene.[7]

In 1981, reports by several researchers were presented which conclusively evidenced that powdered embryonic barley juice will, in vitro (in test tubes), convert such carcinogens as benzpyrene, TRY-$P_1$ and TRY-$P_2$ as well as $P_2$ and 2-amino anthracene into non-mutagenic substances.[8]

Barley juice definitely contains elements which, by decomposing and dissolving these mutagens, can reduce the risk of your having to share space with tobacco smokers and can help prevent cancer and counteract mutations in already damaged DNA.

If you work around exhaust fumes, industrial chemicals, dry-cleaning fluids, pesticides, or other substances of these sorts, the best thing you can do for yourself is to take a teaspoon or two of dried barley juice a day.

## BARLEY LEAVES: DETOXIFICATION CHAMPS

The juice from green barley leaves is definitely one of the best general detoxifiers. It's full of flavonoids which detoxify the cellular tissue as well as polypeptides which can neutralize nicotine and heavy metals, like mercury, into insoluble salts. Everything about it helps to strengthen the organs that purge the bloodstream and excrete the toxins.

Damage to the DNA/genes occurs from various other factors as well: ultraviolet light, cosmic rays, and radiation, for example. Most of these damages can be repaired by natural defense systems, but some get misrepaired while others can accumulate in the genome (a set of chromosomes) due to a weak repair system.[9]

The stronger and more accurate the repair activity in our cells, the better it is for our health and ability to maintain youthful characteristics. Our repair activity gets weaker as we get older, and the damage keeps accumulating. Damage to cellular DNA can relate to the introduction of cancer, allergy, or the death of cells in our body.[10]

## $P_4D_1$ AND DAMAGED DNA: 'NUCLEAR' POWER

A team led by Dr. Yasuo Hotta, research biologist and specialist in gene engineering at the University of California, San Diego, has found that **green barley juice powder has powers which promote the restoration of damaged DNA in the cell's nucleus.**[11]

In one set of experiments, Dr. Hotta's staff exposed groups of human lung culture cells to X rays and others to nitrosquinolin oxide (4NQO, a strong mutagen and carcinogen) to introduce damages (knick and gap formations) onto the DNA. They then divided the cells into two groups one to be cultured with $P_4D_1$, the other not.

Those cells treated with $P_4D_1$ showed a higher incorporation of H3 thymidine into the DNA and mended the DNA's length back to normal much faster, indicating $P_4D_1$ has a stimulating effect on DNA repair. Those cells not treated with $P_4D_1$ fared poorly; many died and the survivors began the self-repair process sluggishly. **Those treated with $P_4D_1$ repaired themselves twice as fast.** But, unless damage was induced, $P_4D_1$ had no effect, indicating that it has no toxicity or tendency to alter uninjured DNA and is safe for healthy cells.

## $P_4D_1$ AND PREVENTION

They found that $P_4D_1$ functioned even more effectively in cells that had been precultured with it, one generation cycle before the induction of damages, in which case the speed of repair more than doubled again.

## $P_4D_1$ AND GERM-LINE CELLS

In a second series, sperm and egg cells which carry all the genetic information for future generations (germ-line cells) were used. The cells which repair these DNA cells are called meiotic prophase cells and, if they are interrupted or disturbed, can cause sterility or birth defects.[12] In these experiments, meiotic prophase cells from testes of older mice were isolated and their reduced repair activity measured. When incubated in $P_4D_1$, a remarkable increase in the repair of DNA was observed.[13] Although this doesn't prove $P_4D_1$ can help prevent birth defects in humans, I believe such biochemical data will soon be forthcoming. From the standpoint of our health, these novel functions of $P_4D_1$ on DNA repair indicate that barley juice has the potential to help protect us from ever-increasing environmental hazards and forced aging, and perhaps even to postpone the natural aging process itself.

## CATALASE AND CANCER

The role of enzymes in cancer therapy is increasing. Green barley juice contains another enzyme which researchers are looking into as a potential therapy — the respiratory enzyme catalase. Dr. Hagiwara explains:

*"Another potential therapy for cancer involves use of a respiratory enzyme called catalase. This enzyme performs an oxidation-reduction activity within cells. During the course of respiration, the cells produce hydrogen peroxide ($H_2O_2$) as a by-product. Hydrogen peroxide has the property of coagulating proteins, and is frequently used as a disinfectant. But, within the body it is toxic and attacks the cells.*

*Catalase decomposes toxic hydrogen peroxide into water and oxygen. Healthy cells necessarily contain catalase. But cancerous cells have been found to contain too little catalase. Unlike normal cells, they are anaerobic, meaning they do not require oxygen in the air or transported by the blood. Instead, they gain energy to metabolize within their own cells. In addition, while normal cells spread, divide, and grow or age and die, cancerous cells do nothing but* grow. *Since cancer cells have such a special energy metabolism function, they do not require catalase.*

*The X-ray radiation frequently used for cancer therapy utilized this property. When the human body is exposed to X-rays, hydrogen peroxide is generated. With healthy cells, catalase acts immediately to decompose it into water and oxygen. However, the cancerous cells which possess hardly any catalase cannot decompose the hydrogen peroxide, but are destroyed.*"[14]

An experimental report suggests that milk may reduce catalase activity in the body fluids. When experimental rats were fed on a diet high in cow's milk, an apparent loss of catalase activity was observed. This would lead to a rise in hydrogen peroxide in the course of metabolism, adversely affecting the cells.

Another experimental report showed that a milk-containing meal also decreased the level of cytochrome oxidase, which is also an important respiratory enzyme.[15]

These reactions are said to occur because of the reduction in iron and copper ions. Catalase is an enzyme having an iron ion, and cytochrome oxidase contains both an iron ion and a copper ion. In other words, these enzymes cannot be formed unless there are plenty of iron and copper ions in the blood.

Milk has a low content of copper and iron. This is not only so with milk, but also butter, polished rice, and bleached bread. Too much of these foods can weaken the activities of these important enzymes in our body, resulting in cancer.

Again, before we leave the subject of cancer, there's a last facet of barley juice I want to mention, concerning a group of substances called mucopolysaccharides which are attracting worldwide attention for possible value in immunological treatment of cancer. Barley juice has been found to contain large amounts of mucopolysaccharides, making it a food with real power.

## SUPER-OXIDE DISMUTASE: A 'SUPER-SPECIAL' ENZYME IN GREEN BARLEY JUICE

Researchers around the world are busy investigating a host of recently discovered practical applications for super-oxide dismutase (SOD). SOD is available under the trade name SODEX. Now a much more potent SOD tablet is available under the name "Superzymes." I like this name for it signifies exactly what the product is — a super-special enzyme with a high potency of SOD.

It is interesting to note that SOD from plants has been found to be considerably more stable, in the body, than SOD obtained from the liver of cattle. Also, since the liver is the detoxifying organ and many cattle are injected with steroids to build muscle tissue, SOD from plant sources is safer. I like this source of SOD because Superzymes are made from a plant source.

Before getting into the details of the functions of SOD, let me give you a background of information that hopefully will help you to see the significance of this enzyme. To date, scientists have discovered three or four kinds of SODs in human tissue; they are found mostly in the liver, erythrocytes (red blood cells), and neutrophils (a "good guy" type of white blood cell). They have been isolated from a wide range of bacteria, blue-green algae, fungi, plants, fish, birds, and mammals.[16] For our purposes, all three SOD forms will be considered as one enzyme SOD.

Research has clearly shown SOD's major role in human nutrition is to fight devastating effects of superoxides, the chemical name for a host of villains called "free radicals." Superoxide radicals are simply oxygen molecules (or atoms) with an extra negative charge on their outer ring, due to an unpaired electron.

This change in the oxygen molecule makes it very unstable — it "goes crazy" and, with great force, begins to bump into other cells and tissues, causing damage of great consequence. It can even penetrate a cell, causing damage to the DNA (part of the genetic code which tells a cell how to normally reproduce itself), producing what is called mutations or damaged cells.

## YOUR BODY'S DEFENSES AGAINST FREE RADICALS

The body has several mechanisms by which free radicals can be transformed back into a stable oxygen and semistable hydrogen peroxide. The process by which this happens is called dismutation. The ways this can happen are these:

- By glutathione — a polypeptide, formed by the body combining three natural amino acids (all are present in green barley juice).
- By anti-oxidant vitamins C and E, with selenium.
- By SOD superoxide dismutase.[17]

Because free radicals have an unpaired electron, they will attack any molecule in your body. Organ or tissue damage occurs when the production of free radicals exceeds that of the scavenger enzymes — the defense system in the cells of almost every organ in the body. These enzymes act like fire extinguishers, designed to put out the free radicals that otherwise burn other tissues or molecules and damage cells by bursting them or rupturing their membranes or by damaging their components.

## PUT THE SOD SQUAD TO WORK FOR YOU!

**SOD's chief function**, in contrast to other enzymes, **is as a cell protector.** It is a powerful free radical scavenger that ferrets out and destroys the hazardous active forms of oxygen that are constantly being produced as chemical by-products of cellular metabolism in the course of respiration and digestion.

You can see, therefore, that superoxides, or free radicals, are the "bad guys" and the natural nutrients, including superoxide dismutase, which destroy them are the "good guys." As this discussion unfolds, you will see clearly the importance of our having a good supply of SOD in our bodies, especially if we are ill with one of the **diseases related to a free radical problem.** Some of those diseases are **heart problems, arthritis, cancer, leukemia, allergies, and lupus.**

Digressing from the usual style of reporting, I am listing here all of the functions of SOD, that I believe there is adequate research to support, and will then give you the bibliographical references. SOD has been shown to:

- Reduce the inflammation of arthritis.
- Aid in the healing of wounds.
- Greatly aid damaged heart, kidney, intestines, pancreas, and skin tissue.
- Reduce the number and severity of abnormal heart rhythms, called arrythmias.
- Act as a cell protector, a main function.
- Reduce chances of getting cancer and a host of other degenerative diseases.
- Slow down the aging process.
- Alleviate symptoms related to radiation sickness.[18]

Dr. Joe McCord of the Departments of Medicine and Biochemistry, Duke University Medical Center, showed that the synovial fluid in an inflamed joint was protected by the presence of endogenous (within the cell) SOD. It was possible to produce, with adequate dosages of SOD, a nearly complete inhibition of the breakdown process. It is well known, of course, that a deterioration of synovial fluid is a symptom which characterizes all inflammatory types of arthritis.[19]

### SOD ACCELERATES HEALING

Robert J. Boucek, M.D., Loma Linda University Medical School, reported, at a symposium in 1984, that superoxide dismutase prevented superoxide radicals from accumulating in damaged tissue, because they underwent a dismutation reaction and were destroyed by the SOD.[20] In plain English, this means that SOD aids in wound healing. Dr. Boucek's scholarly work took 16 pages to report and was most challenging to my best efforts at interpretation. Let me tell you a true story, however, that you will appreciate.

## PRIZE-WINNING PROJECT

In 1986, an Indiana high school student won the state prize with a science project in which her mother, who is a nurse, helped her show the effects of the use of green barley juice on wound recovery time.

An incision was made on the stomach of two experimental white mice. One was given green barley juice to drink and also had daily atopical applications of the powdered green barley juice on the wound. The control mouse had neither of these treatments. The mouse who had the green barley treatment healed more quickly, more completely, and with no apparent complications — in comparison to the mouse without green barley. So, while this study might not meet the standards of a biological research grant given by the U.S. Public Health Department, it was quite impressive for the public to see! The bottom line was obvious — something in green barley facilitated healing. I believe it was the SOD, the chlorophyll, and other nutrients that made the difference!

Another study on wound healing was reported in the Harvey Lectures, Series 79, by Dr. Irwin Fridovich of Duke University's Medical Center — one of the nation's leading experts in SOD research. This study was in relation to tissue damage that results when a surgeon has made a temporary interruption in blood flow to a tissue during surgery. When this is done, as in heart surgery for example, there is tissue damage which occurs because of a lack of oxygen to the cells. This causes the production of free radicals. Dr. Fridovich says that several reports, where experimental animals were used, substantiated his results.

He goes on to say that injected superoxide dismutase has been seen to reduce the size of damaged tissue (the infarct) and in turn activates the neutrophils.[21] Myron Weisfeldt's group, of the Johns Hopkins School of Medicine, reports these same results. He goes on to say that, "As drugs go, SOD is extremely benign (harmless); it could be easily utilized without side effects."[22]

## SOD MINIMIZES TISSUE DAMAGE

SOD catalyzes the dismutation reaction of the superoxide anion and converts it into hydrogen peroxide. This has practical implications for heart attack victims. Researchers in the Department of Medicine at St. Louis University found SOD greatly aids in the maintenance of damaged heart tissue.

After a heart attack, cellular energy production is severely lowered. Prevention or delay of irreversible cell damage can be achieved by simply administering enzymes specifically aimed at maintaining the energy supply of the cell. SOD is one of these enzymes that increases the efficiency of energy production.

Dr. James M. Downey, a University of South Alabama physiology professor has shown that, **by giving SOD to dogs that have had artificially induced heart attacks, the size of the heart attack can be decreased by more than 50 percent.** In other words, the amount of heart muscle that dies can be reduced.

Dr. David Hearse at St. Thomas' Hospital in London has presented preliminary data which show that in rats the use of SOD or similar agents can greatly reduce the number and severity of arrythmias — abnormal heart rhythms. If SOD works in humans as it has in the animals, it could dramatically reduce the death rate from heart attacks, cut the death rate from open-heart surgery, and increase the heart's functional capabilities afterward.

For the past two years, Johns Hopkins University has been in the forefront of animal studies which show SOD eliminates or greatly reduces tissue damage, not only in the heart, but also in the kidneys, intestines, pancreas and skin. **Dried barley juice is an excellent natural source of SOD.**

## SOD AND DNA REPAIR

Another component of the cell that free radicals can damage is DNA. As noted, current theories hold that both cancer and aging result when genes fail to repair themselves. SOD is thought by many to have much the same effects as $P_4D_1$ on DNA prophase cells. In the studies by Dr. Hotta, he found that the repair rate was not as rapid when the cells were incubated in isolated $P_4D_1$ as when they were incubated in plain barley juice — which is also one of the richest plant sources of this enzyme.

Another study that was reported in the *Environmental Health Perspectives Journal* confirmed the work of Dr. Fridovich. Drs. Puglia and Powell of the Department of Pharmacology of the Medical College of Pennsylvania said, "All cells that utilize molecular oxygen ($O_2$) for metabolic or respiratory purposes are at risk of being damaged by activated oxygen (free radicals). In mammalian systems, SOD activity tends to be highest in tissues that have high $O_2$

utilization." Work with mice, they say, "suggests that the function of SOD is to prevent toxic cell damage from a normal metabolic by-product of $O_2$"[23]

## SOD: FREE RADICAL DEFENSE

It is clear from these and many other studies that SOD protects the cells from free-radical damage. In fact, Dr. Fridovich believes from his research that he can say that SOD has a high degree of specificity for $O_2$ in vivo (within the body) as well as in vitro (in test tubes) and that a wide variety of deleterious side effects can be diminished or eliminated by superoxide dismutase.[24] It is obvious then, why, as free radicals are broken down intracellularly, our chances of getting a whole host of diseases are diminished. We are protected!

## SOD, FREE RADICALS, AND AGING

SOD has also been used in research for at least the past 20 years in an effort to understand its deterring effects on the aging process. Since it is known that free radicals damage cells and damaged cells begin to die, contributing to aging, could it be that the SOD could reverse the aging process? Many studies have concluded that it can and it does.

A biophysicist at the National Institute of Aging, Richard Cutler, is one of those who believes it is possible to increase people's life spans by 5,10, or even 15 years — and healthy years at that!

While on the subject of aging, let me stress that aging begins in cells and tissues which are denied the nutritional support they need for reproduction, for repairing the damage done daily by toxins, by poisons, dyes, chemicals, carcinogens, radiation, illness, lack of enzymes, and the lack of oxygen and water.

**Dried green barley juice is nutritional therapy for so many of these cell problems. Its excellent balance of vitamins $B_1$, $B_2$, $B_6$, $B_{12}$, nicotinic acid, vitamins A, E and C, as well as a wide spectrum of minerals, certainly offers a nutritional impact on cell and tissue health while protecting the body against aging and a shortened life span.**

It is well evidenced from research that aged animals have lower activity of SOD than young ones. A study done by Dr. Richard Cutler, a biophysicist with the National Institute of Aging, has shown that life spans of many mammalian species, including man, were directly proportional to the amount of SOD they contain. The species with longest life spans were found to have highest levels of SOD.[25]

Pursuing the implications of this, molecular biologists examined several strains of the same species of mold and recently discovered that those that live the longest are those richest in SOD. This is intriguing, for if a cell's SOD content can be increased, might not life spans be commensurately extended?

Current research by molecular biologist Kenneth Mundres and his colleagues, at the University of Wisconsin, is doing much to bolster the theory that SOD actually can delay or slow down the aging process.

Consequently, as the role of this enzyme has become increasingly understood, SOD has come very much into vogue. In fact, I have read some speculations by certain health enthusiasts who think that by "bathing their cells" in this "fountain of youth," they'll be able to prolong their lives indefinitely, and so forth.

While it may prove true that SOD can delay the aging process somewhat, science will never find an ultimate cure for either aging or death. We die because a mortogenic factor was introduced into our race by a man named Adam and SOD can't change that fact! However, there is every indication that SOD can provide a better chance of a decent quality of life into advanced old age.

**There are also studies to support the value of green barley juice in giving support to cells that have been damaged by radiation.** All forms of radiation produce free radicals, including excessive exposure to the sun (such as I see so often in my home state of Arizona), to computer and TV screens, X rays, food irradiation, microwave ovens, and fall-out from atomic waste.

Clearly, sources in our enzyme family, especially SOD, glutathione peroxidase, methione reductase and catalase, are the most powerful antioxidants our body uses as a first line of defense to fight radiation free radicals. Fortunately for us, nature has a cure. The answer lies in the quality and quantity of our nutrient intake from all sources, including enzyme supplementation.

## SOD AND TUMORS

The last subject under this section is that of the inhibition of tumor promotion by superoxide dismutase. An extensive list of impressive research that has been reported in scientific and medical journals, both in the United States and abroad, reports findings which conclude that SOD can inhibit certain biochemical biological responses, "which strengthen the arguments for an essential role of oxygen radicals in the promotion stage of carcinogenesis and SOD or SOD-like compounds in the homeostatic prevention of carcinogenesis."[26]

## GREEN BARLEY: A SUPER SOURCE OF SOD

In conclusion, it is indeed wonderful that **nature has provided us with a food — barley leaves — which has the power, through enzymes and co-enzymes (in addition to amino acids, minerals, chlorophyll, etc.), to provide our cells with the basic weapons needed for both health and fighting disease.** The decision to incorporate a teaspoon or two of dried barley juice into your daily diet would be one of the best (and most economical) ways to assure yourself of an improved quality of life. Barley leaves are truly food with real enzymatic power!

## CHAPTER X

# Vitamins and Minerals in Green Barley Juice

## Vitamins: Balanced and Naturally Chelated

We are all becoming increasingly aware that we need sufficient amounts of all the vitamins. Often those foods which are naturally high in vitamins do little good when consumed in processed form because vitamins can be altered during processing.

For example, the iron component will change under heat to iron oxide, not easily absorbed by the body. To treat anemia, iron preparations containing iron reduced to this form are popular but not very serviceable for blood formation. Since green barley contains iron in the organically bonded state (divalent iron), it can be immediately absorbed from the intestinal tract.

I want to stress that vitamins in green barley have not been isolated and then recombined, but are, rather, still in their natural (chelated) form, bonded to other nutrient factors as nature created them. Throw together similar amounts of isolated or man-made chemicals, and you will NOT produce the same effect.

## BARLEY LEAVES CONTAIN VALUABLE CAROTENE

There is growing evidence through research to show that, as someone said, it would be "cool" for us to learn to "hang out" daily with carrots and green vegetables. Scientists are saying it this way: "Beta-carotene protects phagocytic cells from free radical damage. It increases the production of T and B lymphocytes and enhances the ability of macrophage, cycotoxic cells and natural killer cells to reverse tumor and cancer cell growth."[1]

And guess what! All of this is without any damaging side-effects. If you eat too much beta-carotene, which is practically impossible, there is a recipe in the cell for getting rid of the excess without any cell, tissue or organ damage. That's more than you can say for synthetic drugs, eh?

Research done with rats showed that infections of the ear, bladder, kidney and gut were prevented and/or reversed when adequate amounts of beta-carotene were included in the diet. Young children with chronic ear infections always showed improvement with increased intake of dietary carotene.[2]

I wonder why M.D.'s today use antibiotics (with their high cost, high health risk and low cure rate) instead of beta-carotene? Is it one more illustration of the failure of modern medicine to acknowledge God's provision for health and healing as superior to their own? It will be interesting to see if we, in America, will ever be privileged to have our doctors acknowledge that nutrition is the foundation of both of these.

How much beta-carotene do you need every day? Authorities differ in their answers, of course. A study done at the University of Arizona at Tucson showed that a single 30 milligram capsule of beta-carotene (equivalent to the amount in about six carrots) reversed pre-malignant leukoplakia in more than 75 percent of the patients without producing any toxic side effects.[3]

Most authorities agree that a DAILY serving of one-half cup of a deep-green leafy vegetable (collards, turnip greens, kale, spinach) or a serving of a deep-yellow vegetable (sweet potatoes, squash, carrots) is considered adequate for good health.

Since powdered barley leaves have generous amounts of beta-carotene, it is one more reason to take one to two teaspoons daily. That would certainly go a long way toward meeting our beta-carotene need in an inexpensive "instant food" way.

## THE VITAMIN BANDWAGON

Many health enthusiasts have gone "vitamin crazy" in the past couple of decades. While I don't doubt that many have experienced immediate beneficial results, one needs to be careful not to go overboard in order to avoid side effects. Even vitamins, especially isolated vitamins, can throw off the body's balance.

Hypervitaminosis, caused by excessive vitamin ingestion, is almost always associated with **synthetic vitamin preparations, hardly ever with natural vitamins.** Since green barley contains vitamins in their natural state, its use will not result in an excessive intake of any particular vitamin.

For example, excess vitamin A can be harmful, but only pure vitamin A in high quantities. Carotene in green barley is called provitamin A, and it becomes vitamin A only as acted upon by the body. It cannot cause hypervitaminosis.

Green barley is an excellent source of live, natural vitamins and is sufficient, I would say, as one's only food supplement. But if you are accustomed to taking more vitamins than in green barley, you might want to continue your regular dosage right along with the green barley. Personally, I continue to take two multivitamins as I always have and also 1 to 3 teaspoons of green barley a day and feel better than I did with the multivitamins alone.

## QUALITY: MORE IMPORTANT THAN QUANTITY

Whichever way you go, I recommend taking only vitamins extracted from food, not synthetic ones. I'm fully aware many synthetic vitamins appear in the lab to be no different from those extracted from nature, but I remain suspicious that what they do in a test tube and what they do in my body might not be the same.

Ultimately, the safest and surest source of good nutrition is from grains, legumes, vegetables (including green plants), and fruits. Adverse effects inevitably follow ingestion of large quantities of unnatural food of unbalanced organic-inorganic nature.

Included for your study is Table 6, comparing the vitamin content of dried juice of young barley leaves with that of several popular foods.

**TABLE 6**

### COMPARISON OF THE VITAMIN CONTENT OF GREEN BARLEY ESSENCE (5 gms.) AND SEVERAL POPULAR FOODS (Average Servings)*

|  | Vit. A (I.U.'s) | Vit. B1 (mg.) | Vit. B2 (mg.) | Vit. C (mg.) |
|---|---|---|---|---|
| **Vegetables** | | | | |
| Barley Green | 287 | .029 | .049 | 4.2 |
| Broccoli | 1,940 | .070 | .155 | 70.0 |
| Brussels Sprouts | 405 | .060 | .110 | 67.5 |
| Cabbage | 95 | .030 | .030 | 75.0 |
| Corn | 330 | .090 | .085 | 6.0 |
| Green Beans | 340 | .045 | .055 | 7.5 |
| Peas | 430 | .225 | .090 | 16.0 |
| Potatoes | trace | .075 | .035 | 15.5 |
| **Fruits** | | | | |
| Apples | 40 | .030 | .020 | 2.0 |
| Bananas | 145 | .040 | .045 | 7.5 |
| Oranges | 180 | .090 | .035 | 45.0 |
| Peaches | 1,130 | .015 | .030 | 6.0 |
| Pineapple | 55 | .070 | .025 | 13.0 |

*Green barley values taken from *Green Barley Essence* Yoshihide Hagiwara, M.D. All other values taken from *The Agricultural Handbook #56*, "Nutritive Values of American Foods in Common Units," The Agriculture Research Service, United States Department of Agriculture, 1975.

## MINERALS: ALL OF THEM

All living organisms are born and die with minerals as their axis. Man was made from clay. Burn a plant or a man and you get the same minerals in the ashes. Unlike plants, however, the human body cannot draw necessary minerals directly out of its environment or manufacture them. Our only source is in food we eat.

Among other functions, minerals maintain the pH balance in our bodies. When we lose our acid-alkaline balance, our cell metabolism suffers. This can lead to all sorts of trouble. Our cells maintain this balance by constantly absorbing, consuming, and discharging various minerals.

Enzymes, agents that make metabolism possible, work only if the right minerals are dissolved as ions in our cell fluids. All chemical changes within our cells require enzyme action, and minerals have so much to do with the action of enzymes that they may be called the enzymes for the enzymes!

When the right minerals are not present in an ionized condition, most enzymes cease functioning effectively, often completely. When foods with proper mineral content are neglected, or when foods with high concentrations of the wrong minerals are consumed heavily, the body cannot prosper.

## WHERE HAVE ALL THE MINERALS GONE?

The American diet is short on minerals because it is short on vegetables and grains. The skeleton of a man who died today would yield less potassium and other minerals than the skeleton of a man who died at the turn of the century.

Not only do we eat fewer mineral-rich foods, but those we eat are of diminished mineral content. "Factory" farming methods, besides polluting the soil with industrial chemicals, bleach it chemically of its inherent energy. Also, nitrogen compounds are released as never before into the air by automobiles and industry, where they change to nitric and sulfuric acid (acid rain).

This "acid rain" is progressively dissolving the alkaline metals in our soil, robbing it of potassium and magnesium and other minerals essential to the vitality of all forms of life. Most of the fruits and vegetables we buy today have been grown in such soil by such methods and are consequently of a much diminished vitality from those of even 50 years ago.

## SALT: NATURAL AND PROCESSED

Also, we tend to be getting way too much of certain minerals like phosphorus and, especially, sodium (salt). Two grams daily of salt is sufficient for human beings, but most of us consume 10 times that much. What makes it worse is that the salt we use today is made by ion exchange membrane methods and is a reagent-grade chemical, 99.9 percent pure sodium chloride. Natural salt contains bittern with minerals like potassium, calcium, and magnesium that are absent in our modern product.

A fish that will live for a week in the solution mentioned above, will die in a few hours in a solution made from what's in our salt shakers today. Salt exerts great effects on our cells, and the mineral deficiency in our present species of table salt should be regarded as a serious matter. I believe it is linked to our loss of health in general, and, especially, to the increase in heart disease, hypertension, and fatigue. Pay the extra pennies to put the natural sea salt we used to use back on your table. Even so, nearly all of us eat too much salt.

## HIGH IN POTASSIUM

Green barley is very high in potassium which works to balance this sodium excess. Let's focus on this. Potassium is especially important because it has a very high ionizing tendency. It is consumed incessantly within our bodies in the process of energy metabolism. When potassium levels fall too low, osmotic pressure of the cell membrane is disrupted. To adjust osomotic pressure, sodium and other ions take potassium's place in the cells.

As long as these potassium ions are continuously supplied, there is no problem. But if the potassium supply fails, sodium increases above a healthy limit. Naturally, the balance of ions within the cell fluid is disrupted. Some enzymes continue to work, but others falter or stop functioning altogether.

Modern diets tend to foster this condition because the proportion of acidic foods (such as meat, starch, and sugars) is large, and that of alkaline foods (primarily vegetables and fruits) is minor. Over-consumption of acidic foods, with only small amounts of potassium, is involved in a broad range of disease conditions.

Many have attributed high blood pressure, heart disease, and circulatory disease partially to over-consumption of salt and high sodium levels. It has been found, however, that many drugs that alleviate high sodium levels also tend to deplete the body of potassium, so the result may be lowered blood pressure or fatigue, because of potassium lack. Research shows that, if potassium is simply added to the diet, it balances and neutralizes the sodium levels and helps to lower the blood pressure.

## HYPOKALEMIA: NOT ENOUGH POTASSIUM

Hypokalemia results from a reduced potassium concentration in the blood. Symptoms include body languor (weakness), especially muscular fatigue, and can lead to paralysis. Furthermore, cirrhosis hepatitis is, in a sense, a disease associated with loss of potassium. Also, many medicines lower our potassium level dangerously. When a diuretic or cortisone is administered, excretion of potassium from body fluids increases abruptly. Dr. Hagiwara says when such a therapy is practiced, potassium in a completely natural form should be supplied at the same time.[4]

Also, the motion of muscles involves a release of potassium. Our heart and blood vessels continue to contract and relax from birth to death without a moment's rest. What happens if potassium is not supplied sufficiently for the working of your heart and blood vessels? The muscles strongly resist releasing potassium, and if the potassium deficiency is exacerbated by continued consumption of acidic foods containing much fat but few minerals, cholesterol and wastes build up in the blood vessels.

Heart diseases of the middle and old-aged, such as myocardial infarction, mostly afflict those who eat luxuriously and seem to be exposed to much stress. Stress itself also involves a release of potassium. Potassium in green barley can help improve these conditions and serve to prevent heart disease.

How could all these diseases be related to something so simple as a lack of potassium, you may be wondering. Well, your automobile might provide a good analogy. It's made to run with five quarts of oil. Insist on operating it with two quarts and you'll eventually ruin everything from the water pump to the wiring (and lots of things in between). Our bodies are like that. Deny the whole body what it was meant to "run on" and it will eventually start breaking down all over.

The first sign of potassium shortage is usually fatigue. The fatigue that attends strenuous physical exertion and mental activity, or stress and the fatigue following lack of sleep differ metabolically, but they all share one common denominator — a build-up of sodium and loss of potassium. Too much salt or too little potassium will result in tension and muscular fatigue.

Dr. Hagiwara asks, "What happens to those who continuously follow a diet deficient in potassium?" Since the body has a self-defending system, there will be an effort to store potassium within the cells. If complete loss of potassium is threatened, the body tries to prevent secretion of potassium. Consequently, our bodies are forced to stop all strong muscular exercise.

"Exertions of the brain or nerves, which consume greater energy than physical labor, become dull. This in turn causes the body to stop releasing potassium and results in sleepiness and languidness. If you noticed this and took potassium, the cells would regain vigor and resume energy metabolism."[5]

If you are always tired, try green barley and see if it doesn't make a difference. I have eaten "right" for years, yet it gives me more energy — and I believe it will help you as well.

## PHOSPHORUS BALANCER

The other mineral we get too much of is phosphorus, especially phosphoric acid. In experiments where mice are fed calcium and phosphoric acid in varying ratios, as the amount of phosphoric acid increases, so do occurrences of bone malformation. Increased phosphoric acid in the feed of pregnant mice produces a proportional increase of malformed fetuses. **Stay away from phosphoric acid, and, most especially, from fizzy soft drinks.** They're refreshing for the moment, but they're trouble in the long run. Give them up and don't let your children drink them. They will ruin teeth and bones and upset other calcium functions.

For example, hypocalcemia is a disease resulting from the reduction of calcium concentration in blood. It manifests itself in bone troubles, osteomalacia, abnormal excitation of nerves, or a disordered condition of the parathyroid gland. I can't prove it, so I'd better not say what my suspicion is about the cause of Kaschin-Beck disease, but, please, most especially if you're pregnant, AVOID PHOSPHORIC ACID!

So many of the foods we eat, including meat, are high in phosphorus and low in calcium. Green barley is the reverse and can help balance out the surplus phosphorus, promoting better utilization of all minerals. A deficiency in any one mineral will upset our ability to profit from the others. (For example, both hypokalemia and hypocalcemia can be induced by the deficiency of a magnesium ion in body fluids.)

Dried barley juice has a wider range, higher quantity, and better balance of minerals than any of the foods that are commonly valued for mineral content. Because of the small percentage of kelp in it, green barley also has trace amounts of all the 14 other minerals, including molybdenum, iodine, germanium, selenium, and lithium, all in their raw organic forms.

Dr. Hagiwara explains, "In raw vegetables and meats, minerals are bonded in an organic form to enzymes, proteins, amino acids and sugars inside individual cells. Scientifically, these are called organically bonded (chelated) minerals. But, upon heating or freezing, silicic acid, phosphoric acid, and other compounds intrude upon those minerals' bonds, converting the minerals into an inorganic state which is not easily absorbed." Again, the minerals in green barley have not been freeze-dried and are still in their original, easily absorbable, biochemical form.

Included for your study is Table 7 which compares the mineral content of green barley with several popular foods.

**TABLE 7**

**COMPARISON OF THE MINERAL CONTENT OF GREEN BARLEY ESSENCE, (5 gms.)
AND SEVERAL POPULAR FOODS (Average Servings)\***

|  | CALCIUM | PHOSPHORUS | IRON | SODIUM | POTASSIUM |
|---|---|---|---|---|---|
| **VEGETABLES** | | | | | |
| Barley Green | 55.4 | 29.7 | .79 | 31.0 | 445.0 |
| Broccoli | 68.0 | 48.0 | .60 | 8.0 | 207.0 |
| Brussels Sprouts | 25.0 | 56.0 | .90 | 8.0 | 212.0 |
| Cabbage | 32.0 | 155.0 | .20 | 10.0 | 118.0 |
| Corn | 2.5 | 73.0 | .51 | trace | 136.0 |
| Green Beans | 31.5 | 23.0 | .40 | 2.5 | 95.0 |
| Peas | 18.0 | 79.0 | 1.50 | 1.0 | 157.0 |
| Potatoes | 4.5 | 32.0 | .40 | 1.5 | 221.0 |
| **FRUITS** | | | | | |
| Apples | 4.5 | 6.5 | .20 | .50 | 69.0 |
| Bananas | 6.0 | 19.5 | .56 | 1.0 | 278.0 |
| Oranges | 37.0 | 18.0 | .35 | 1.0 | 180.0 |
| Peaches | 7.5 | 16.0 | .45 | 1.0 | 172.0 |
| Pineapple | 14.5 | 6.5 | .40 | 1.5 | 122.0 |

\*Green barley values taken from *Green Barley Essence*, Yoshihide Hagiwara, M.D.,Table 8, Page 50.
All other values taken from The Agricultural Handbook #56, "Nutritive Values of American Foods in
　Common Units," Agriculture Research Service, United States Department of Agriculture, 1975.

## CHAPTER XI

# Research: The Foundation Stone

Yes, it's true. You can fool all of the people *some* of the time and some of the people *all* of the time, but you cannot fool *all* of the people *all* of the time.

Millions of Americans are searching for the truth about how to achieve a higher quality of health than they presently enjoy. Why? Because their experience with modern methods in medicine have caused them to conclude there *must* be other alternatives for their health problems.

My readers in this country and abroad already know my bias, learned in the Nutrition Research Laboratory at Ohio State University's Medical School in the late 1930's. As a student worker there, I gave the mice their food and beverages and kept their cages clean. From that experience, I concluded that Mr. Food Doctor does indeed exist.

Time and experience with more laboratory mice, as well as with people, have only strengthened my beliefs. In fact, you can put my name on the side of two famous M.D.'s of centuries ago:

"Thy food shall be thy remedy" — Hippocrates (460-370 B.C.).

"To live by medicine is to live horribly" — Carl Linneaus (1707-1778).

### WHERE IS THE EVIDENCE?

You may be asking: "Where is the scientific evidence for this position? Show me double blind studies."

All right. I am ready.

At his full-time research center, the Hagiwara Institute of Health, Dr. Yoshihide Hagiwara of Japan and his fully trained M.D.'s, gene engineers, and other medical professionals concentrate solely on researching green barley leaf juice, made into a powder.

If the following evidence convinces you of the benefits of green barley, I suggest you experiment with a daily intake of Dr. Hagiwara's product composed of field-fresh barley leaves grown on organic soil without pesticides or chemicals of any kind. Who knows? You may want to add a testimony of your own to the millions of us who have come to appreciate the benefits of improved health.

Let's look at some of the results of Dr. Hagiwara's more than 25 years of research.

## SKIN DISEASES

A study conducted at the Muto Dermatologic Hospital in 1977 included 38 patients ranging in age from 10-47 who had been undergoing treatment over a long period of time or who had suffered recurring bouts of their diseases.

These skin diseases included:
* *Acne pustulosa* — skin filled with pus or lymph.
* *Chloasma* — patches of skin discolored by yellowish or brown pigment.
* *Facial melasma* — discoloration of the facial skin.
* *Eczema* — chronic inflammation of the skin.
* *Seborrheic eczema* — a disease of the oil secreting glands.
* *Atopic dermatitis* — inflammation of the skin.

In addition to their skin diseases, nine of the patients had other conditions. These were: diabetes, chronic urticari (nettle rash; itching), gout, multiple pelade (loss of hair in patches), acyesis (female sterility), fever of unknown cause, constipation, pityriesis capitis (dandruff), and leukoplakia (white patches on the cheek).

Thirty minutes before each meal, these patients received a heaping teaspoon of green barley juice (Barley Green) three times a day, dissolved in water. If the condition warranted it, the dosage was increased to two teaspoons (6 gms.) before each meal.

Four to 12 weeks later the results of the skin experimentation were compared with the first examination of the patient.

## THE RESULTS

Reading the individual case histories of the patients is fascinating, but space does not permit detailed elaboration of the results of this project. The summary research statement, however, provides the outstanding results:

> *Green barley juice was given to patients with 29 types of skin*
> *diseases and 9 other types of diseases. The ratio of successful treat-*
> *ment was 75.5% in skin diseases and 81.6% in all cases.*
> *Particularly good effects were noted in atopic dermatitis [inflam-*
> *mation of the skin]. In all cases, no side effects were observed.*[1]

When the patients discontinued taking green barley juice, there
was minimal effect on recurrence of the conditions. This supports the
writer's belief that a teaspoon or two of green leaves of barley per day
would enhance and help to sustain excellent health throughout life.

## A PERSONAL WORD: LIVING PROOF

As a teenager, the wife of my former pastor had an extreme case
of acne pustulosa. Later, her face healed but not without ugly scar-
ring.

She was in her 40s when I suggested barley juice powder by Dr.
Hagiwara as a nutritional support of her general health. *(Hereafter,*
*the symbol [n.n.], for "no name," will represent the brand of green*
*barley juice used in these studies.)* Immediately upon starting her
new regimen, her face began to have many "zits" — or small eruptions of pus.

She phoned me and asked if this condition could be caused by the
green powder. My answer was, "Yes, but keep on taking it."

She did. Within six months she phoned again to say that her complexion was the best it had ever been in her adult life — and there has
been no recurrence of the acne pustulosa.

Another women wrote to me saying that from age 17 her facial
skin had what the doctor diagnosed as cystic acne and had taken
antibiotics for years. One year after using [n.n.], she gave up the
antibiotics and gradually over a four-year period, she says her skin
has become as smooth as a child's and some of the wrinkles have
gone, particularly around her eyes. *(D.S., Ohio)*

## ENDURANCE: ON THE RUN

In addition to the positive results in treatment of skin diseases,
green barley juice can also affect how well and how long our muscles
move.

The Science University of Tokyo conducted a study to demonstrate whether or not the effects of green barley juice on endurance
and motor activity could be also found in experimental animals as
was purportedly shown in humans. The [n.n.] was offered by Japan
Pharmaceutical Development Company, Ltd., Osaka, Japan.

The dried barley leaf juice [n.n.] was added to the standard food for mice at the 2% and 4% levels. The foods were maintained under ideally controlled laboratory conditions for both temperature and humidity.

The control group of mice were fed only the standard diet for mice while the test group were given either a 2% [n.n.] or 4% [n.n.] addition to the standard food diet.

To test motor activity (muscle movement) in mice, a wheel cage was used as the testing instrument. The number of revolutions of the wheel cage were recorded 30 minutes after placing the mice in their cages. The test lasted for two hours.

The method of feeding the mice to test for endurance was similar to that described above. The mice from both the control group and test groups were placed on a tread mill; they were required to run at a rate of one kilometer per hour with an uphill slope of 17 degrees, being forced to continuous running with stimulation of electric shock of 80 volts.[2]

## ANTI-FATIGUE

The results were clear. The [n.n.]-added food statistically significantly increased the motor activity in mice — as would be expected if the mice had been stimulated by caffeine or amphetamines but without central nervous system stimulation. The results showed that the increase in the motor activity in [n.n.] fed mice was not induced by central stimulants. Thus it can be concluded that the [n.n.] fed mice showed anti-fatigue activity as has been so often reported in humans.

The effects of [n.n.] on greater endurance in mice was also statistically significant and dose related. Those mice on 4% [n.n.] food showed more endurance than the 2% [n.n.] food mice. Both of these groups, however, had more endurance than the control mice.

Data also revealed another fact. Seven days feeding of [n.n.]-added food failed to significantly prolong the mice's forced running time, but 15 days feeding *did* prolong their endurance. This shows us not to expect instant results.

One last fact emerged from this study. The average body weight of mice fed on [n.n.] food was larger than mice fed on standard food. It would appear that the [n.n.] might be nutritionally better than the standard commercial diet for mice.

How can we apply the results of this study to the human condition regarding motor activity and endurance? From the testimonies of thousands of people regularly using green barley leaf powder, I believe it is fair to conclude that the increased muscular activity and increased physical endurance of [n.n.] users when contrasted with the general population can be substantiated by this Science University of Tokyo study.[3]

## A PERSONAL WORD: WORLD CLASS ENDURANCE

It is my opinion that thousands of people who are regular users of the green barley juice powder produced by Dr. Hagiwara have experienced a surge of new energy that endures throughout the day and evening hours.

An outstanding example of this comes from the testimony of Harry Sneider, Ph.D., an exercise training specialist in Resistive Rebounding and the 1995 champion world class weight lifter in his age category (54 years).

In 1984, when Dr. Sneider began taking the [n.n.], he increased his own world champion weight lifting score by 49 pounds.

He recently told me that not only does [n.n.] give him stamina and endurance, but it boosts his recuperative powers. He said, "It seems to produce a kind of healing effect in my whole body after a weight-lifting event."

As a body builder and weight-lifting expert, Dr. Sneider trains athletes for Olympic competition in six different events. For further details, Dr. Sneider can be reached at (818) 355-8964.

## HIGH CHOLESTEROL

Many people today are concerned about their cholesterol levels, especially those diagnosed with hypercholesterolemia — excessive cholesterol in the blood.

Several authors associated with the Hagiwara Institute of Health in Hyogo, Japan, did a study to find and identify substances in green barley juice that display anti-hypercholesterolemic activity.

This study demonstrated for the first time that two substances found in green barley juice — hexacosyl alcohol and B-sitosterol — when suspended in olive oil and added to a high cholesterol diet in a one percent concentration and given orally to the mice or rats had anti-hypercholesterolemic activity. At the same time, the administration of these barley juice fractions in a dose of 10 grams per kilogram revealed no detectable toxic effect in the mice.

The authors of the study were not able to determine the exact mechanism at work to achieve these results. Attempts to clarify the mechanism of the hypo-cholesterolemic action of hexacosyl alcohol, however, are underway.

The final conclusion of this study "suggests that [n.n.] might be very useful in preventing vascular diseases associated with hyper-cholesterolemia in humans."[4]

## A PERSONAL WORD: SHOCKING HEALTH CHANGES

One morning as I passed my neighbor's apartment, I could see through the screen door that he was working on his computer. I also noticed that his face was very flushed, so I took two steps backward and asked, "Bill, are you all right today?"

He answered, "I just started taking a new blood pressure depressant and am feeling dizzy." Bill went on to say that his father had died at age 55 with heart problems and now at age 50, he was experiencing some of the same symptoms as his dad.

The day before, his doctor had just completed Bill's blood work which indicated his blood pressure was 220/120; his cholesterol was 320; his triglycerides were over 400; and he was 45 pounds overweight.

When Bill showed me the laboratory's results, I asked, "Would you like to improve your health by making some nutritional changes?"

Bill answered, "Yes, I would."

I gave him some literature to read, including copies of my own books.

After three weeks of adding [n.n.] and making some dietary alterations — less meat, eggs, cheese, milk products, and eating more fruits, vegetables, and whole grains — Bill returned to his doctor to see how the new regimen was working.

Bill's next blood test showed that his blood pressure was 165/85; his cholesterol was 185 (perfect for men); his triglycerides were down to 250; and he had lost five pounds. (Today his cholesterol is in the 165 range.)

The doctor was shocked and exclaimed, "What in the world have you been doing? You are the best you have been in the five years I have been your doctor!"

## GROWTH RATE, SERUM CHOLESTEROL, ETC.

In another study, eight groups of male and female mice composed of 25 in each group were fed, under controlled laboratory conditions for 450 days, one of three standard foods: 1%, 2%, or 4% dried green barley juice added to standard laboratory animal food. The control group of mice was fed only the standard food.

The body weight of the mice was measured every two days. The internal organs of each group were under close observation as well as measurement of each mouse's weight. The serum cholesterol level was also determined after six months of feeding.

The results? The [n.n.] barley powder accelerated the growth rate in both the male and female mice; however, the addition of the [n.n.] did not produce obesity. In fact, the serum cholesterol level was significantly lowered. Moreover, special substances that inhibit the intestinal absorption of cholesterol were found in the green barley juice powder.

The authors ended their discussion of this study by stating: "Thus, dried green barley juice is considered to be a health food of special interest from not only nutritional but also from pharmacological points of view."[5]

### ANTI-INFLAMMATORY PROTEIN FROM BARLEY LEAVES

Another positive nutritional aspect of green barley juice concerns health problems related to inflammation that causes swelling in various parts of the body.

A paper, published in the Japanese *Journal of Inflammation*, established the fact that green barley leaf juice exerts extremely strong anti-inflammatory activity.[6] Several factors in barley leaf extract have anti-inflammatory properties (i.e., SOD, $P_4D_1$, $D_1$-$G_1$, which are protein fractions). At the same time, no toxic signs were evident when administered orally or subcutaneously — even at very high doses.

Since any condition that produces swelling, heat, pain, and a possible loss of normal function involves inflammation, it seems, therefore, that barley leaf extract would have a significant application in a wide variety of conditions involving inflammation. (See Chapter IX for a more detailed description of this subject.)[6]

### A PERSONAL WORD: THREE CASES IN POINT

Although I have received many personal testimonies regarding anti-inflammatory situations, I will include in a few words only three.

"I have my four-year-old son taking [n.n]. He has suffered from bronchitis since he was born and has always had ear and throat infections during the winter months. He no longer has bronchitis, and it has been four months without a single ear or throat infection. Even his teacher at the day care center is bragging about his attitude and behavior changes."

A second situation comes to mind involving a chronic case of cystitis (bladder infection). A young girl with this condition had been on a number of different drugs, but each time the symptoms recurred. The girl's mother wrote: "[n.n.] gave her complete relief."

Lastly, a letter from a woman with debilitating arthritis told how she had to have one knee replaced. Two years later, however, arthritis had set in with swelling and crippling effects. In addition, her left elbow, right shoulder, and feet were swollen and painful. She couldn't even wear her shoes. Her letter says, "Two weeks after I started taking [n.n.] the swelling was gone, the pain was gone, and I can wear my shoes."

## ANTI-ULCER ACTIVITY

In another study, researchers set out to determine whether or not juice from young barley leaves could prevent peptic ulcer formation in the stomach of rats. Four methods of inducing ulcers were used: stress, aspirin, acetic acid, and shay rats (a type of rat prone to ulcers).

This study showed that green barley juice contains a variety of substances that reveal significant anti-ulcer activity. It appears that the barley juice fractions do not themselves attack the ulcer. Instead, the effect of green barley juice on the movement and flow of blood in the stomach and the defense ability of the stomach mucosa are associated with anti-ulcer activity.[7]

My files contain a number of letters telling about the healing of ulcers after a few weeks of [n.n.]. One such letter read: "We wanted you to know that we have started taking [n.n.] and our health has greatly improved. No more colds or flu, and my wife has stopped taking her Tagamet since her ulcer seems to have completely disappeared. We no longer get headaches, and we sleep much better."

## RELEASING THE GROWTH HORMONE

In 1994, four major research centers made a significant discovery about green barley leaf extract. Published in the *Journal of Nutritional Biochemistry,* this study was conducted by the Department of Biochemistry and Molecular Biology of George Washington University in Washington, D.C.; the Department of Physiology of the Medical University of South Carolina; the Department of Microbiology of the University of Virginia, Charlottesville; and the Hagiwara Institute of Health, Hyogo, Japan.[8]

Previous to this study, it had been reported that green barley leaf extract contained one or more molecules that enhance the release of the hormone regulating prenatal and postnatal growth and/or prolactin. The hormone prolactin initiates or sustains the function of secreting mother's milk in mammals. These substances are both released from the anterior pituitary — a small endocrine gland at the base of the brain that secretes hormones influencing body growth and also affects metabolism and the functioning of other endocrine glands.

The objective of the 1994 studies was to identify the molecule(s) in green barley leaf extract responsible for stimulating the growth hormone and lactation hormone beyond their normal range of functioning. With the aid of a newly developed procedure using liquid chromatography, it was possible to isolate and chemically analyze the biologically active molecule.

The molecule was identified as "a-tocopherol succinate," an analog (a structurally similar compound but different in one molecule or radical) to "a-tocopherol" or vitamin E. These studies are the first to document a role for vitamin E in regulating growth hormone and prolactin release, suggesting that this vitamin may also have an important role in regulating growth and lactation — an heretofore unknown function.

The components found in green barley leaf extract, therefore, can affect not only fertility but the development of the baby in the womb and the growth of the child during breast feeding.

When my niece was having trouble getting pregnant, I suggested she change her fast-food diet to a more nutritious one and also try taking [n.n.].

"You'll be pregnant within a few months," I said.

She followed my advice, and recently gave birth to a healthy baby girl.

## BARLEY LEAF EXTRACT INHIBITS TOXIC ALDEHYDE

In 1993, researchers isolated a new isoflavonoid in green barley leaf extract. Named 2-O-glycosylisovitexin (2-O-GIV), this flavonoid was shown to have strong antioxidative activity. It inhibited what is called lipid peroxidation, a harmful intermediary process that can occur during the digestion of fats that have been overheated in processing or cooking.

The bad news for North Americans is that we consume large amounts of these overheated fats. We also consume large quantities of fats that have heated to the smoking point — like barbecued products from the home grill — or that have been subjected to day and night heating — such as occurs in the cooking of French fries in fast-food restaurants .

Such fats are rendered unfit for proper digestion and/or assimilation. They can form toxic compounds, one of which is known as malonaldehyde. Examples of the harmful effects of these denatured fats are: DNA damage (causing genetic "accidents"), cancer, early aging, alteration in plasma membranes, damage to enzymes, etc.

Now the good news. In the 1993 study, 2-O-GIV in green barley leaf extract was shown to stop the production of malonaldehyde. By one procedure, 2-O-GIV inhibited its formation by 99%; another method inhibited it by over 90%.

We now have a known method for protecting ourselves from the toxic compound malonaldehyde: regular ingestion of generous amounts of young barley leaf extract — the one used in this study.

Further research for application of 2-O-GIV to actual pharmacological practice is in process.[9]

## CONTROLLING PANCREATITIS

Osamu Yokono, M.D., of the Department of Medicine of the University of Tokyo, conducted a study to determine if a water-soluble form of chlorophyll-a and related substances in young barley green juice could be successful in the treatment of patients with chronic pancreatitis. In this study, chlorophyll-a was used in two ways — by intravenous injection and by oral use of the spray-dried extract of young green barley leaves.

This study sought to answer the question: Can a decline in the length and severity of the disease at it beginning or at the recurrence of inflammatory symptoms be observed?

The results of this study showed:

- Out of the 34 patients with chronic pancreatitis involved in this study, 23 cases showed "fairly favorable effects" and 9 cases were assessed as having "somewhat favorable effects."
- The main disturbing symptom of pancreatitis, abdominal pain, disappeared in a week or so with the infusion of 5-20 mg. of chlorophyll-a per day for one to two weeks.
- When the disease recurred, all patients could be well controlled by intermittent administration of chlorophyll-a.
- There were no side effects in all the cases treated with chlorophyll-a — no allergic, photosensitivity, or liver toxic symptoms of any kind.

The conclusion is clear: The administration of the spray-dried extract of young green barley leaves give some favorable effects on the pathological phenomena associated with chronic pancreatitis.[10]

## PHARMACOLOGICAL ACTIVITY

Young barley leaves have been known to possess potent pharmaceutical activities, including anti-oxidative activity, anti-inflammatory effects, and anti-allergic activity. The name of this flavonoid is 2-O-glycosyl isovitexin (2-O-GIV).[11]

"Flavonoid compounds, which are widely distributed in the plant kingdom and occur in considerable quantities, show a wide range of pharmacological activities other than their anti-oxidative characteristics. These substances have been used to treat various pathological conditions including allergies, inflammation, and diabetes. In fact, the experimental data showing their high pharmacological activities such as anti-viral and anti-tumor is accumulating; their therapeutic potential, however, has not been fully proven clinically. The investigation of the pharmacological potency of flavonoid compounds would provide evidence for their possible use in therapeutic treatments."[12]

A personal word. While the present-day medical profession can hardly tolerate patients giving their anecdotal success stories (they want only scientific proof) there has now accumulated a wealth of testimonies showing the efficacy of green barley leaf extract. It appears that cells of all kinds respond favorably to generous amounts of barley juice powder. Yes, I have come to highly respect the power of this extraordinary food concentrate.

## THE FINAL WORD

Three additional studies which are included in Chapter IX of this book are an important part of Dr. Hagiwara's research program. The subjects deal with the anti-tumor promoters from edible plants, the prevention of aging and adult diseases, and the stimulation of DNA repair by novel components of barley extracts. Make sure to read again the outstanding facts revealed by these studies.

One final conclusion is easy for me to write: I believe there is probably not a close rival to the nutritional and pharmacological power of Dr. Hagiwara's young, raw, green leaves of barley powder.

It appears to me that the Creator of all things has given us another perfect illustration of His exquisite design — the perfect plan for self-healing of most of modern man's ills by the ingestion of the gramineous (of the grass family) plants, so easily available in the form of BarleyGreen.

And remember this: all living, rejuvenating, healing processes are ultimately related to the work of nutrients — the kind that are present in generous amounts in barley leaf powder as produced by Dr. Yoshihide Hagiwara.

The whole world serves as a proving ground for this concept.

## CHAPTER XII

# A WORD
# TO READERS

As we told you in the foreword, our main purpose in writing this book on the dried juice of young barley leaves is to encourage Americans, and people everywhere, to improve their declining health through improving their diet.

Believing as I do that the best, easiest, quickest, least expensive single way of improving the nutrient density of your diet is by the daily addition of a serving of green leaves of barley, I have done my best to introduce you to the scientific facts about it. Hopefully many of you will also want to read my book entitled, The Spiritual Roots of Barley. It adds a deep dimension to the subject of barley.

The next step is up to you. It is obvious that making wise food choices and providing nutritious meals for yourself and family has a price tag attached. But remember this: NEGLECTING to get serious about your nutritional health has a much higher price.

More than a year of my life has been invested in writing this book. If as a result of reading it, you take the positive steps to improve your diet, write to me and share what you have done— what changes you have made. My address is: Dr. Mary Ruth Swope, P.O. Box 5075, Scottsdale, Arizona 85261.

## FOOD POWER IN ACTION

### DEAR DR. SWOPE

Come into my study and read over my shoulder for a while. Some remarkable "coincidences" have happened to people taking green barley. That marvelous self-healing system known as the human body will astonish you with its rapid and efficient response to nutrient-dense foods like green barley juice. When we supply that system with all the crucial nutrients in the right amounts, then we can watch it do just what it was designed to do—produce vibrant health and strong resistance to disease.

You have heard me say before how firmly I believe in the restorative powers built into the human system. Let me share with you how and when that belief happened.

### HOW I LEARNED ABOUT THE 'FOOD DOCTOR'

It all began soon after enrolling in my first course in nutrition, when I was a sophomore at Ohio State University.

Students were assigned to cleaning the rat cages in OSU's Medical School Nutrition Research Laboratory, and I was no exception. (This was before the mainstream of medical science abandoned nutrition as a viable way to promote and/or restore health.) It was there that I observed the differences in the physical characteristics of mice being fed different rations.

I could see, even without any formal education in nutrition, that the mice who were denied vitamin A had weak eyes with crusty matter on their eyelids and masses of corruption in the corners. Unlike the thick, glossy fur of the "perfect diet" group, these mice had thin, dull fur, and their sharp claws left marks on their skin from constant scratching. They were thinner and obviously in an overall poorer state of health.

It was equally obvious, without reading the nutrition textbook, that the symptoms were from a lack of each of the nutrients under study. The amazing thing was that when the missing dietary nutrient was supplied in proper amounts, in just a few days you could hardly tell the difference between the once sick mice and those who had always had a "perfect diet." That really taught me a lesson I've never forgotten—there truly is such a thing as a "food doctor."

To me, the REAL "Food Doctor" is Mother Nature. The perfect plan for the sustenance of man and other animals was put into place before man was even created. (That story is told in Genesis, Chapter 1.)

It is my belief that no amount of denying these obvious facts, or even passing legislation in an attempt to wipe out the concept in favor of a "better way," will ever diminish the truth. The truth is, of course, that **the body is self-rejuvenating, self-healing, self-energizing, and self-renewing.**

"Doctor Food" will always outperform "Doctor Drugs" as a disease preventive and as a force in maintaining excellent health.

"Doctor Drugs" can save our lives in time of crisis, but they are not the source of wellness. It is a wide variety of natural foods which is the source of the broad spectrum of nutrients required by the body for growth, maintenance, and repair of body tissue.

Remember as you read, that no claims can be made for green barley as a "cure" for any specific disease or condition. Something much more profound is going on here. I invite you to share the experiences of some who have chosen wholeness through the daily consumption of juice made from green barley leaves.

## RESEARCH PROJECT:
## OPINIONS OF SELECTED CUSTOMERS OF
## DRIED BARLEY JUICE

From the medical and nutritional research literature, as well as my own experience in animal research laboratories, I learned, years ago, something I've never questioned or forgotten. It is easy to produce clinical changes (sickness) in animals through malnutrition and it is equally as easy to produce rapid and dramatic recovery (cures) through returning good nutrition to the poorly nourished animals. In other words, what symptoms poor diet causes, excellent diet reverses. Nutrients can and do turn sick cells into healthy cells. Millions of us can attest to that.

Believing as I do, I selected the brand of green barley powder that is one of the most excellent sources of raw, organically grown, unprocessed, alkaline-ash, very nutrient-dense food, and began to take it. Being able to "feel the difference," I began to share it with others.

After hearing so many good remarks about the product from a few people, I wondered if it produced any profound clinical changes in other users. Intrigued by this thought, I set out to answer the question: Does the addition of green barley to one's daily food intake have any observable effects on health?

A questionnaire was developed and administered to 205 persons who had been continuous green barley customers for one year or more. These customers represented both sexes, a wide variety of ages and were from many parts of the country.

## SUMMARY OF QUESTIONNAIRE RESPONSES AND LETTERS

There were 120 individual responses in our survey. Approximately two-thirds were made on questionnaire forms sent out by the author, and one-third were unsolicited letters of testimony.

Of the 120 respondents, 102 reported positive results from using it, and the majority of these gave detailed accounts of specific symptoms which disappeared after starting to use the product.

Twenty respondents with positive results had those results confirmed by their doctors. Five respondents reported an improved level of health and well-being with no change in specific symptoms. Eleven reported no change, and two reported some mild digestive upset with no improvement of symptoms. We heard of detoxification symptoms ranging from mild to severe from about one-quarter of the group, with positive results.

The disease for which symptomatic relief was most often reported was arthritis—25 respondents mentioned it. Next in frequency were reports of lowered blood pressure. There was a tie for third for improved eyesight, improved skin texture and cancer remission. In all, respondents mentioned 99 different symptoms improved after taking green barley.

It is interesting to note that about one in ten felt they were not helped. In my opinion, this is most often due to a lack of understanding of what to expect when people improve their diet. As detoxification begins, they misinterpret the signs and quit taking the product. Too, it probably has more to do with biochemical individuality than with any particular condition, since no particular pattern of symptoms proved consistent.

[Note: Hereafter, this symbol [n.n] ("no name") is being used to represent the brand of green barley juice represented in this study.]

## DISCLAIMER

Unsolicited testimonies as well as those secured through the administering of a questionnaire are included solely for the purpose of nutrition information and education. Nothing in this book should be construed as medical advice.

Products made from raw, young, green barley leaves in the form of barley juice powder have no medical properties. They are not, therefore, intended for the cure, mitigation, prevention, or treatment of any disease, illness, or symptom.

Please consult your physician or other qualified health professional should your health problems warrant the need for onc.

## CHAPTER XIII

# My Customers Speak

*This chapter contains excerpts from letters I have received since the first edition of* Green Leaves of Barley *was published. Some have been mildly edited for better readability. For documentation purposes, each letter has been given a number followed by the initials or the city and state of the writer. The symbol [n.n.] for "no name" represents the brand of green barley juice used by our customers.*

### FAST FOOD OF THE FUTURE

We are grateful for [n.n.] — the fast food of the future — because it has enabled us to have a zest for life.

As a nurse, I have always been interested in nutrition and health. I was skeptical about [n.n.] even though I had heard stories of unbelievable health reversals. What [n.n.] gives is a smorgasbord of super nutrition to feed the body and replace damaged cells.

It has equipped our high energy family with a better immune system so we rarely get sick. My leg cramps disappeared, and the PMS symptoms are a thing of the past.                              *253, K.C.*

### FEELING "HIGH"

I got excited about [n.n.] after only a few days of taking it and felt so "high" that I began telling all my friends about it.

The arthritic pain I had in my fingers at that time is now completely gone. My skin is now smooth on my forearms. It used to be quite rough.

I am forever grateful.                              *201, Brookings, Oregon*

## NOTHING TO LOSE

I had a bone scan, X-rays, and lab work showing I had cancer in the lymph nodes throughout my body. When I refused to have chemotherapy, my doctor told me to go home and stay on pain pills. Some friends told me about [n.n.], and I made an appointment to show it to my doctor. After reading the literature and seeing [n.n.], he said, "You have nothing to lose and everything to gain."

When I started taking [n.n.], I had been on 20-26 pain pills 24 hours a day. After 10 days, I began to feel a difference and took fewer pain pills.

After two months, I returned to my doctor who took more X-rays and suggested we compare them with those taken two weeks before I started on [n.n.]. He found I was in complete remission! At that time I was only taking four pain pills a day, and since then I have not taken any. I am feeling great!                                    *202, R.S.*

## HAPPY AND FULL OF ENERGY

After a spinal fusion operation for two ruptured discs in my neck, I had to wear a heavy back brace and became severely depressed. I resorted to anti-depressants, which helped but had severe side effects — weight gain, hard to wake up, etc. I weaned myself off them and fought the depression for nearly a year.

Then the Lord led me to a woman whose husband had been taking [n.n.] for three years for manic depression and was now doing wonderful. I've been taking [n.n.] for five weeks, and I feel reborn — happy! I'm so full of energy. I jog two miles every day and my neck does not hurt anymore. [n.n.] has renewed my body and mind so I can be the Christian I am meant to be.                                    *203, J.K.*

## TOO GOOD TO BE TRUE?

At 37, I had multiple health problems and had undergone numerous surgeries, including a total hip replacement. Facing surgery on the other hip because of intolerable pain, I went to my orthopedic surgeon who put me back on the anti-inflammatory medication, Feldene.

That very same day, a friend told me about [n.n.]. It sounded too good to be true, but I was willing to try it. That was a year ago, and I never did open the bottle of Feldene.

I am totally free of pain — no more migraine headaches, sleepless nights, or upper respiratory infections, not even a cold. And I have quit my allergy shots, too. I will still need to have that second hip replaced some day, but I'm sure that is a long way off now.

*204, J.K.*

## NO MORE WARTS

I started taking [n.n.] about three months ago, and after about six weeks I couldn't believe my eyes when I realized that two warts I had on my right hand fingers had completely disappeared.

The one on my thumb had been there for over 20 years, and a doctor had burned it off once but it came back. I still rub my fingers together amazed to see them normal after so many years.

*205, Calexico, CA*

## THE END OF ALLERGY SHOTS

*A young boy wrote that he and his mother had allergies:*

The things that made me sick were dust, pollen, and oak trees. I had to have shots every week so my nose wouldn't run. I often got respiratory infections with high fevers. I was always pale with dark circles under my eyes, and I couldn't gain weight. I hated food, and Mom would cry sometimes because I wouldn't eat.

Mom started me on [n.n.], and pretty soon I started feeling better. I didn't seem to catch colds as often. After eight months, Mom and I quit taking our allergy shots — and I just keep getting better.

I think I would have become very sick, sooner or later, if my Mom hadn't cared enough about me to force me to take [n.n.]. Now if she forgets, I ask her for it. I'm not a shrimp anymore either, and it sure feels good not to be sick all the time. *206, Two Harbors, MN*

## CYSTS GONE; THYROID NORMAL

I just want to praise God for giving me [n.n.]. After taking three teaspoons a day for three weeks, my doctor could not find any cysts in my breasts. All pain and soreness were gone.

After three months, the doctor tested my thyroid gland, and it is working normally for the first time in seven years. I don't have to take Synthroid any longer. Also, my blood sugar is more stable, and my allergies are better.                                    *207, Valparaiso, FL*

## MORE ALIVE

I have been using [n.n.] for four months, and it has cleared up a long-standing gall bladder disorder, digestive disturbances, chronic constipation, and a lifetime of athletes feet.

I am 58 years old and have more energy and feel more relaxed and alive that I have for many years.        *208, Nashville, TN*

## IMPROVED SKIN CONDITIONS

A friend and I decided to use [n.n.] as a facial mask. We mixed 1/2 teaspoon of [n.n.] with 2-3 drops of water, forming a paste and smoothed it on our face. After letting it dry for 10 minutes, we washed it off with water.

Within a day or two, we both experienced a smoother, clearer complexion than we had before. My dry skin became moist, and I stopped using a moisturizer at night.

I then had other people work on their own "problem" areas. A fifteen-year-old boy had his acne clear up after about 4-5 days. A woman, who had blotches and burns on her arms associated with multiplesclerosis, had her arms heal in four days, even though dermatologists had been unsuccessful in the past.

A man who had skin cancer had previously had some areas burned off. He had used creams on these areas for two years, but they were still red. He put [n.n.] paste on twice one afternoon, and the redness went away.                                    *209, Kettering, Ohio*

## TESTS NORMAL

My sister had aplastic anemia, requiring blood transfusions every two months for 13 years. After a few weeks on [n.n.], she was tested and her blood count is normal!                          *210, F.E.*

## NO WITHDRAWAL SYMPTOMS

At 23, I was an alcoholic, and my life was a shambles. I knew I had to stop drinking. I had tried to stop before, but I went through the shakes, vomiting, and insomnia. Finally, I quit drinking and began taking [n.n.] three to four times a day — and I had *no* withdrawal symptoms.

I had also had high blood pressure for most of my life. In two months, my blood pressure went from 150/90 to 95/60. This is the lowest it has ever been, and I feel the effects of it.　　　*211, C.F.*

## NO LONGER BED-RIDDEN

I have systemic lupus, a chronic inflammatory disorder of the connective tissues caused by a breakdown in the auto-immune system. I was bed-ridden or too sore to move for the last nine years, limiting any activity to a maximum of about 40 minutes.

After my husband and I began taking [n.n.], my neighbors wondered how I had so much energy. Some of my friends did not recognize me after I was on [n.n.] two months. In fact, one man thought I had died and my husband had married a younger lady!

I still have to pace myself, but now at least I am able to do things. My husband feels like a new person also.　　　*212, I.H.*

## IMMEDIATE RELIEF

Two years ago, I was sick with a virus infection and arthritis. I was taking a pain killer for the intestinal tract, and Tylenol to help the arthritis, all the while becoming more helpless. Then a friend insisted [n.n.] would help all my problems.

Each morning I would take [n.n.] and received immediate relief. Soon I ceased having the problems altogether and never did take another pain killer tablet.　　　*213, B.P.*

## A HEALTHY FAMILY

My husband and I began taking [n.n.] and in about six weeks found tremendous changes in our health. For him it was a bad sinus condition every fall, which always ended in infection.

When he was out of town, we forgot to send [n.n.] with him, and the fifth day, he began to have sinus problems. He started taking [n.n.] again and to date has had no sinus problems.

In my case, my nerves are now calm, and I have no more sleepless nights or tired spells during the day. Also, hot flashes and aching joints are gone. A cystic tumor, which a doctor has monitored for three years, has completely disappeared.

Our grandchildren are taking it, and this has been the most healthy year our whole family has ever had. **214, R.M.**

### A WILL TO LIVE

About six and one-half years ago, I began to notice an unusual tiredness and lack of energy. I was either cold or too hot and suffered severe muscle spasms. After being examined by eight individual physicians, it was found that I had a tumor on the pituitary gland. Both the gland and the tumor were surgically removed.

Three years later, I had my gall bladder removed, suffered severe stomach problems, and developed esophagitis. Heart problems led to a triple by-pass, and two years later I was found to be mildly diabetic and suffering from rheumatoid arthritis. I was taking 19 prescriptions every day.

A friend sent me a jar of [n.n.], and in a short time, I began to regain strength and energy as well as a will to live. My stomach aches quit, the severe muscle spasms stopped, and I lost about 16 pounds of excess water weight. I am now able to work 12 to 14 hours a day, and presently take only six medications.

My doctor is aware that I am taking [n.n.] and has no objections. I cannot say that [n.n.] is a sure cure for any illness, but I will say it is the only change I made in my oral intake prior to my improvement in health. **215, J.L.**

### BLOOD COUNT NORMAL

At ten years of age, our daughter was diagnosed with leukemia and put into remission with chemotherapy, but the disease returned. Her doctor told us that if they could put her back in remission, she might live another year. If not, she might live only six months. He felt the leukemia had become immune to the chemotherapy.

Every time she took chemotherapy, her blood count would fall very low, and she would have to miss treatment for several weeks. She also lost her hair.

Within the first week of taking [n.n.], her hair started to grow back, and her blood count came back up to a normal range. Her blood platelets rose as high as 520,000 — normal counts are from 150,000 to 500,000. She has not had to miss one chemotherapy session. They said this is very unusual.

Her bone structure had been so damaged by the leukemia that the doctor compared her bones to those of a 70 or 80 year old person, and she had to wear an upper body brace 23 hours every day. Now she no longer has to wear it.

Our daughter has been healthy and full of life with lots of energy, especially since she started on [n.n.]. We know [n.n.] has made a world of difference for her. *216, R.E.*

## HOT FLASHES AND BACK PAIN

I have been using [n.n.] for the past four or five months, and the hot flashes I was having due to change of life have disappeared, making life much more pleasant for me and my family. I had been waking up as much as ten times a night from the hot flashes, and it was causing me to lose a lot of sleep.

For 40 years, my back was giving me much pain. Just before I started taking [n.n.], I said to my husband, "If my back continues getting worse, I will soon be a cripple."

After six to eight weeks on [n.n.], I noticed a drastic change and seldom ever feel any effects from my back problem now. *217, M.T.*

## FEELING 16 AGAIN!

When I was rushed to the hospital, thinking I was about to have a heart attack, the doctor did numerous tests and found that my liver enzymes were double what they were supposed to be. My nerves were a mess, and I was deeply depressed. I told people I felt as if I were 90 years old.

A friend told me about [n.n.], and I started taking it. In three days, I felt 16 years old again! My husband and children were amazed and thought they had a new wife and mom. My outlook on life has changed.

After receiving the results of my last blood test, my doctor is all for [n.n.], and said, "I don't know what you've done, but keep it up."

**218, K.V.**

### LIVER SPOTS VANISHED

I have been taking [n.n.] for more than a year, and it has helped clear up my complexion. All my brown liver spots have vanished from my hands.

I also use [n.n.] as a facial masque, and it has pulled out many ingrown facial hairs.                                **219, Calgary AL**

### A NEW LEASE ON LIFE

Before taking [n.n.], my blood tests were not so good. My cholesterol was too high, but the last test showed dramatic improvements without taking any medication. I am now in the superior category for my age group.

My strength has increased, and my lung function is above normal. My hair has become thicker, and my nails have grown long for the first time. My allergies are gone, and I am free of an acid stomach and have no more digestive problems.

My vision has also improved, and my dental check-ups are the best ever. I am saving money on mouthwash because [n.n.] gives fresh breath. My skin has become soft, and my hysterectomy scar has almost disappeared. My blood pressure is outstanding and has come down since my last physical.

I feel I have a new body and a new lease on life even though I spent many years with a lifestyle that damaged my body. Who knows how far [n.n.] will take me!                                **220, A.D.**

### A CLEANSED SYSTEM

Not only has [n.n.] made me feel better than ever, but it also began a process of cleansing my system of built-up toxins.

After taking [n.n.] for eight weeks, I noticed a strange-looking oval blister near my naval. The next day, I was broken out over my stomach, back, head, and face. This unusual manifestation turned out to be a classic case of chicken pox. My mother told me I was exposed many times as a child to this disease but never had it.

It appears that [n.n.] literally flushed the disease out of my system! At age 51, I finally caught up with the other kids.  *221, J.M.*

### NO TRACE OF ULCERS

When I got sick, my doctors told me I had ulcers all the way up into my esophagus. I was also diagnosed with diverticulosis, a hiatal hernia, and painful diarrhea.

I've been on [n.n.] for more than a month, and my pain is all gone. The doctor says I have no trace of diverticulosis nor any ulcers. The diarrhea is absolutely gone, and even the hiatal hernia has relaxed so my swallowing and vomiting have improved and vanished.

I am well and have never felt so wonderful!  *222, I.J.*

### CALMED NERVES

After using [n.n.] for only one week, I can already report what it is doing for me. My nerves are calmer, and I feel less stress at my job as a school teacher. The muscles in my arms are stronger, and I move faster.

My sinuses are more clear, and my hot flashes are gone. I have more energy although I sleep fewer hours. My agoraphobia appears to have left me, and I feel younger!  *223, S.T.*

### NORMAL EYE PRESSURE

We have been taking [n.n.] for about two months. My husband has been borderline glaucoma for about 15 years, but he just had a completely normal eye pressure test!

Our son has been taking thyroid medication. Since using [n.n.], his most recent test was so outstandingly different that his doctor in disbelief called for a repeat examination.

My fingernails are getting stronger, and I have never had such durable nails.  *224 E.A.*

## WALKING WITHOUT LEG BRACE

My family and I were in a near fatal car accident, and I was severely injured by the lap belt. My aorta was severed, which affected all the nerves and muscles in my right leg. I developed arthritis in the ankle bone on top of my foot and have had to wear a leg brace to walk.

A friend gave me your book and a bottle of [n.n.]. Within four days of taking two teaspoons daily, I had no pain upon arising, and the swelling and stiffness are better every day. In my home, I can now walk without my brace at times, and my leg and foot are starting to heal.                                          *225, B.C.*

## AS NATURE INTENDED

For 33 years, I have had **aching joints, great fatigue, and cycles of differing pains.** For the first 16 of those years, I went undiagnosed. But tests showed I had **SLE (systemic lupus erethymatosus).**

While some of the medicine kept me alive and functioning in low gear, steroids were damaging my body, robbing me of calcium in the bones and causing bleeding ulcers. The medication I took for high blood pressure stated in the fine print that it could cause SLE, which I already had!

A nurse friend introduced me to [n.n.], and after six weeks, I am now up to one teaspoon twice daily. What a change! The constant joint pain and headaches I'd had for years lessened. I have gradually reduced the pain medication from seven to one per day — and sometimes none. My stroke-level blood pressure is down to 130/82.

I am grateful for the research scientists who have brought this product to the forefront so our bodies can be healed as nature intended.                                          *226, North Rose, NY*

## THE THREE DAY MIRACLE

After I was diagnosed with **bone cancer**, life did not seem worth living to me. Then I started reading Bible passages on healing, and a friend told me about [n.n.]. As people prayed for me, my hope and faith began to grow.

After a few months, I went on a Friday for a pelvic exam and bone scan. The diagnosis was cancer of the uterus and kidney.

Monday I went for more tests. The kidney scan report taken Monday morning showed no cancer! A miracle — from Friday to Monday!

At noon the same day, I had a biopsy of the tumor in the uterus. When I nervously returned on Tuesday for surgery and treatment, I had little hope. Then to my surprise *and* the doctors, the biopsy showed no cancer.

I owe my life to God, [n.n.], and all the wonderful people who remembered me in their prayers.                    *227, Milwaukee, WI*

### NOTHING LIKE IT

This [n.n.] is something very special. My **vision** has improved, and my husband's blood pressure is going down.

**Our dog,** who **had ligament injuries** when we got her, is no longer limping.

My seventy-seven-year-old mother-in-law, whose only remedy for pain relief of arthritis seemed to be **knee replacement surgery,** started on [n.n.], and in *days* decided she might not need the surgery. Previously, she was in so much pain her eyes would fill with tears of discouragement.

I have been taking [n.n.] for almost a year and have never known any other product like it.                    *228, Nevis, MN*

### STRONG AGAIN

When I started taking [n.n.] just 40 days ago, I had **sores on my foot from years of poor circulation.**

Now my feet are healed, and they are not sore when I walk. Also my legs are strong again, and I can walk for three miles without any trouble.

Between [n.n.] and the right diet, I am just great. My whole body feels better.                    *229, R.F.*

## GETS HER LIFE BACK

Before I was diagnosed with **rheumatoid arthritis**, I was very active and working at a very physical job that required lots of walking and working with my hands.

A rheumatologist immediately put me on Prednisone and eventually on several other anti-inflammatory medicines. None of these worked. I gained lots of weight, going from a size 14 to size 20. All my outdoor activities were curtailed because I was told to stay out of the sun.

The inflammation caused carpal tunnel syndrome, and I had to have surgery on my hands. Still the pain, swelling in all my joints — hands, elbows, shoulders, hips, knees, ankles, feet, jaw — got worse. I felt my life had been taken away from me and feared becoming a cripple.

I prayed hard for healing, and God heard my prayers. A friend introduced me to [n.n.], and I began taking it along with eating more fruits and vegetables and eliminating all "trash" foods.

When I had to have a **hysterectomy**, the doctor kept saying, "I can't believe you just had surgery. You look so great — so healthy." I told him what I was doing, and he encouraged me to stick with it.

Since then, I have lost 50 pounds, and am almost off all medications and feeling great! I now play volleyball again and walk three miles a day. My cholesterol reading went from 230 to 161. People even say my complexion is great. It is good to have my life back.

*230, M.B.*

## "THIS MAKES SENSE"

For four years, I had **low blood counts, tumors on my body**, and had been told by my doctor that my **bone marrow damage** was permanent.

I began taking [n.n.], and within four months I watched my hard tumors soften up and melt away right before my eyes. It felt strange not to feel the large tumor under my arm anymore.

When my doctor examined me, he was amazed and asked, "What have you been taking?" I showed him the [n.n.], and he said, "This makes sense."

He immediately sent me to the lab for a blood test. They indicated my blood counts were normal when two months before they had all been depressed. I also had a very painful bone marrow biopsy done, and it showed my bone marrow was completely healthy.

My husband also started taking [n.n.] after he was diagnosed with severe inflammation of the **prostate gland** and hospitalized twice. He has not had another attack of prostatitis in ten years.     *231, J.P.*

## AN ANSWER TO PRAYER

Our daughter suffered for years with **ulcerative colitis** that caused her colon to ooze blood, along with **constant cramping and diarrhea**. One evening after eating pizza, she came home bleeding heavily and in terrible pain. I knew she would have to be hospitalized if something wasn't done.

I made an enema using [n.n.] and gave it to her slowly so it would stay for awhile in her colon. Soon, her pain eased and finally left. Every day after that, she began to drink [n.n.] faithfully and today, ten years later, she has never had another attack of colitis. When she went to the gastroenterologist for a checkup recently, he said he couldn't tell that she had ever had the disease.

Fourteen years ago, my son was diagnosed with **schizophrenia**. Since that time, he had been housed in state hospitals that refused to give him [n.n.] no matter how much we pleaded. Two years ago, he was assigned a new doctor who was willing to write an order for [n.n.] to be given three times a day.

Within three months, our son began to improve, and his illness seems to have stopped progressing. We now have renewed hope for him.

I believe [n.n.] was an answer to prayer for our family, and I am so thankful to God for what it has done for all of us.     *231, J.P.*

## MAKING THE DIFFERENCE

**Problems with my sinuses often led to bronchitis and chest congestion.** A nose and throat specialist suggested opening a blocked sinus and removing a polyp, which a CAT scan confirmed. I was on cortisone, steroids, and many antibiotics.

Since using [n.n.], I have had no sinus infections, much more energy, and a very "up feeling." I also had stomach problems and much gas, but have none now. I know [n.n.] has made the difference.

*232, E.D.*

## SICK ALL OVER

After my wife's death, I became very sick. To control my stomach, I was taking five teaspoons of Mylanta every day. I also had painful **bursitis, arthritis** in my hip, and **no energy**. I was sick all over.

A blood test showed I had almost no white blood cells, and doctors prescribed seven drugs. I spent every day counting the pills and keeping up with the medications but didn't feel any better.

When my brother suggested I try [n.n.], I told him I was already taking enough pills to choke a horse. He insisted and told me it isn't another medicine or chemical; it is a food — a concentrated balance of 23 minerals, 16 vitamins, 18 amino-acids, and live enzymes.

Within two months, my blood count was normal, my stomach calmed down, and I cut out all Mylanta. My bursitis and arthritis quit hurting. Today I am full of energy and way past 70 years of age. I am no longer sick. I take an aspirin occasionally, but I take [n.n.] every day.

*233, J.D.*

## PATIENT TEACHES NURSE

I had been **crippled with arthritis for years**. Although I had one knee replaced, two years later arthritis set in and became swollen again. My left elbow and right shoulder were swollen and painful as were my feet, making it impossible for me to get my shoes on.

I wore large, extra wide boots until I got [n.n.]. In two weeks, the pain and swelling were gone, and I can now wear my shoes. It is so good to be without pain and be able to walk around again.

My home health care aid was so pleased with my improvement that she told the RN and her administrator about me. As a result, several women from the regional home health office came to see me, and they all bought a jar of [n.n.].

The nurse said, "We go to school for years to learn to be a nurse, then we go to one of our patients and she teaches us how to get well."

*234, V.A.*

## NOT TOO LATE

When I was diagnosed with **metastasized breast cancer** that had already spread to three lymph glands, my doctors strongly advised chemotherapy. I refused, and decided to go to Mexico for treatment with nutritional therapy.

When friends told me about [n.n.], I quickly added it to my very strict, highly nutritious diet. Currently, according to a live cell test, there is no sign of cancer.

I personally know several doctors who recommend [n.n.]. It's the best way to keep your body defenses strong, so you can resist disease. But if you do have a degenerative disease, it is not too late to rebuild your body.

*235, J.B.*

## FEELS YOUNGER

Due to breathing chemicals in my work, I have had **digestive problems along with acute gastritis and gall bladder problems**.

In three days after taking [n.n.], I saw a change. Previously, my food would stay in the stomach for days, but no longer.

At 68, I work 40 hours a week and my mind is alert. I have lost weight and feel much younger. The gas problems and gall bladder condition have disappeared.

*236, V.B.*

## REPAIRED HEALTH

I contracted the **Asiatic flu** that swept through our state. After I was introduced to [n.n.], I got results within one week and returned to work when most people were taking two to three weeks to recover.

At the same time, my wife was suffering from **depression and insomnia.** My recovery convinced her, and she took [n.n.]. That night she enjoyed the first complete sleep in three weeks. After three days, she was in a positive frame of mind, and the depression disappeared.

The cells receive good nutrition to make healthy blood, which in turn heals the body and repairs our state of health to normal — which is different for every person. God is using this product to give us what we all need to help maintain our bodies.                    *237, F.R.*

### A LIVING TESTIMONY

For years I was bothered by chest pains and had been unable to sleep on my left side. I spent thousands of dollars going to doctors, but they could not find out what was wrong with me. The last doctor, however, determined that my problems may be a result of a very **acidic system**. He told me to go on a very bland diet and learn to live with my problems.

I have spent quite a few dollars looking for a natural remedy. When I saw the video tape on [n.n.], I was skeptical at first but went ahead and bought a jar.

To my amazement, after only a few weeks on [n.n.], I have not had any more problems with my chest or stomach. I am now a living testimony of how [n.n.] can improve your health.        *238, H.P.*

### LEG PAIN AND GUM DISEASE

As a special education teacher, I often had pain in my legs when I stood or sat for long periods. During summer vacation at my daughter's home, I began taking [n.n.] faithfully. My legs felt better, the varicose veins were normal, and standing for long periods didn't bother me.

Also, the threat of having a gum operation because of **pyorrhea** was relieved when the doctor said I was doing fine. I have been promoting [n.n.] to all my friends, and they, too, are experiencing the value of better health.                    *239, N.W.*

### A BETTER BIRD DOG

My nine-year-old German short hair bird dog started having trouble in her hips. The veterinarian said there wasn't much that could be done for her.

I decided to give her a teaspoon of [n.n.] every day in a small amount of milk. Within a week, she had some relief from her suffering, and her energy level was on the rise.          *240, Cascade, ID*

## THE LAST HEADACHE

I am 62 and have suffered from **chronic headaches** for 40 years. In the last four years, pain from **arthritis** of the spine has been alleviated only by pain killers.

After reading *Green Leaves of Barley,* I began taking [n.n.] and immediately noticed improvement. I also modified my diet, drank eight glasses of water daily, and walked an hour each day.

In exactly six weeks, I was free of arthritic pain except for a minor pain in the fourth toe of my right foot. Three days later I also had my last serious headache. Thanks for writing your book.

*242, S.M.*

## DOCTORS CONFOUNDED

At age 67, I was diagnosed with **bone cancer**. Doctors at the Mayo Clinic believed the mass in my chest had been developing for almost four years and gave me no hope for recovery. They gave me radiation on the bone, but there was no medical treatment for the chest tumor.

I began mixing [n.n.] in my orange juice, and six months later, X-rays showed that the chest tumor had shrunk to half its original size and the formerly damaged bone tissue had been restored 80 percent with heavy calcium buildup. The doctors were confounded and have no answer for what appears to be a miracle.          *243, T.H.*

## "KEEP DOING IT"

My husband has been a **brittle diabetic for over 30 years** and has had many complications, taking large doses of insulin daily, from 80-100 units morning and afternoon.

After taking [n.n.] for a few months, his insulin requirements began to decrease and dropped to 30-40 units twice a day. How thankful we are for this blessing.

His eyes developed **diabetic retinopathy**, which required laser surgery on both eyes but with little improvement. After his last visit the doctor said, "I have never seen your eyes in such good condition. Whatever you're doing, keep doing it!"

His **blood pressure** read 160/130 for years and required medication. After taking [n.n.] for a few months, he is off the medication since his blood pressure dropped to a normal reading of 120/74.

*244, M.W.*

## PUTTING IT TO THE TEST

I had been plagued with **lower back pain, weakness, poor balance, double vision, and lack of co-ordination.** My neurologist ordered a MRI scan, which showed I had multiplesclerosis. I was subsequently termed permanently disabled.

When a friend of my son's introduced us to [n.n.], I was skeptical at first but finally decided to give it a try. I started on a Thursday and by Monday, my double vision had cleared, and my energy level was up so dramatically that I climbed up on the roof of the house to clean the chimney.

Still skeptical that [n.n.] could have made such a drastic change, I stopped taking it, and within three days my symptoms returned. When I started on [n.n.] again, my double vision and weakness cleared up quickly.

Once again, I decided to put it to the test. After a few days, the symptoms returned again, convincing me that [n.n.] was doing the trick.

I recently introduced another M.S. patient to [n.n.], and she had similar outstanding results. Before, she had been taking various types of natural vitamins costing $400 a month, which did not accomplish what [n.n.] did in a short time.

*245, N.P.*

## SURGERY CANCELED

A friend told me that her eight-year-old daughter was **hard of hearing** and scheduled for surgery to have ear tubes inserted and her tonsils and adenoids removed.

I told her to try [n.n.] first. In three weeks, the surgery was canceled.

About six months later, when the child returned to the ear specialist for a hearing test, the doctor was overwhelmed and said she now hears better than most normal people.

More than two years later, the girl has still not needed the surgery, and she no longer has ear infections, colds, or flu.          *246, K.M.*

### "SURE SMELLS GOOD"

When I first started taking [n.n.], I thought it would be a good nutritional addition to my diet. To my great surprise, it proved to be much more.

Within the first week, my arthritic pains began to disappear and energy levels increased. Then I noticed I began to have regular bowel movements, after having had irregular loose movements with cramps for over two years.

My brother also started taking [n.n.]. After two weeks, he came home and exclaimed to his wife, "Supper sure smells good."

His wife turned around in surprise since he hadn't smelled or tasted anything for over two years! His senses have continued to improve, and he is enjoying his wife's cooking more than ever.

*247, M.B.*

### ALL-DAY EXCURSIONS

I began feeding [n.n.] to **our aging cat** who appeared to be afflicted **with arthritis** in his hind legs.

Now he jumps high up on furniture and goes on all-day excursions.          *248, E.M.*

### FEELS FANTASTIC

Before taking [n.n.], I had all the symptoms of **diabetes — vision and kidney problems**. My eyes used to blur when I moved my head, and I could barely see short or long distances.

Now I haven't worn glasses for four years, nor do I need them. I also had many tiny ulcers on my bottom gums, and my **gums bled**

**profusely** for years. In addition, I had **severe menstrual problems** with excruciating pain and excessive bleeding. After I began taking [n.n.], I was saved from having a scheduled hysterectomy.

One of my most embarrassing problems, which had become the family joke, was my **poor memory**. Now I have a lot of energy, mental clarity, drive, and a sense of well being. In fact, I run two successful businesses, home school, teach Sunday school, and feel fantastic.

My husband, who was a chronic asthmatic, now takes no medicine and is healthy and strong.                    *249, K.M.*

## CONTINUED IMPROVEMENT

I was diagnosed with a severe case of **gum disease**. My **teeth were loose**, very tender, and bleeding each time I brushed. The gap between my two front teeth was getting larger by the month, and within a year I had spent $1200 on dentist visits.

Four months after I started taking [n.n.], my dentist said my gums were much improved, my teeth were not loose, the bleeding had stopped, and the gap in my front teeth was narrowing. Every month, I notice continued improvement.                    *250, M.T.*

## A FEW MONTHS TO LIVE

One of our staff women shared that her sister had **cancer** and that the doctors were unable to do anything. They just sewed her up and told her she only had a few months to live. They did give her chemotherapy. She immediately began taking [n.n.] and now has no trace of cancer.

Another woman has an **inoperable cyst** in her brain. Her severe headaches cease when she takes [n.n.].

Two little children suffering from leukemia are at a point of seeming arrest. Their parents are giving [n.n.] to them.                    *V.B., 252*

## CLASSIC "BIG C" CASE

Here is a report written Aug. 10, 1986, by a dear friend of mine:

*You asked for an update on my Auntie's condition; I am happy to oblige. First though, let me share some facts about her case.*

*On April 1, 1986, my 89-year-old aunt and I went to the City of Faith in Tulsa, Oklahoma, for a regular medical checkup. Much to our surprise, Auntie was diagnosed as having an ovarian tumor the size of a small basketball. Later we learned that it was cancer. She was advised to return to her home in Wisconsin for surgery. (At this time, Auntie had been on two teaspoons daily of [n.n] since the previous Dec. 1.)*

*En route home we traveled to a Women's Aglow meeting where we knew there would be many women in attendance who believed in prayer and would pray for us. Little did we expect, however, what happened next. The tumor burst and Auntie nearly died. Three doctors told us the poison from the tumor literally spewed out and covered the liver and kidneys. The prognosis given by these doctors was very grim indeed.*

*On May 2 surgery was performed; on May 9 she came home from the hospital. The oncologist was very insistent that Auntie begin chemotherapy immediately after the surgery. We refused and told him of our interest in using nutrition and prayer as the mediums of healing. After his third try with us, he said disgustingly, "Food never did heal a cancer and it never will." We accepted his opinion but stood firm on our own!*

*At this time, since her April 1 diagnosis, Auntie was taking two heaping teaspoons of [n.n] four times a day. In addition, she was taking 3,000 mg. of vitamin C several times a day.*

*Freshly made carrot juice (8 oz.) was routinely scheduled for each morning and each afternoon and, in addition, she was given two full recipes of what we called, "The Green Drink." Here are the ingredients, which we put in a blender:*

*2 cups of any kind of juice (she liked apple best)*
*2 heaping teaspoons of ground sunflower seeds*
*2 heaping teaspoons of almond seeds*
*2 tablespoons yogurt*
*6 large leaves of romaine lettuce*
*2 tablespoons Shaklee's protein powder*
*1 banana*

*Every day Auntie drank one or more kinds of tea. Too, she took a 20-minute walk every day and twice that amount if she was able.*

*Improvement was almost immediate. I must add, however, that there was much Bible reading and quoting, a great deal of prayer, and much "talk" between us about our confidence in God to heal Auntie. This spiritual food, we believe, was actually more important than the physical food.*

*Another Rx for both Auntie and me was hearing, over and over again, the testimony tapes you sent us. Knowing that they were nurses and understood blood reports, etc., gave us total confidence in what they said. They also gave us the standard we needed for judging Auntie's blood test scores.*

*On May 20 Auntie's blood work gave us a "Praise the Lord" report. Her red blood cell count was 11.6, her white blood cell count was 5,000 and her blood pressure was 160/84 - all within the normal range. Her blood had been improving each test time, but it is wonderful to have it totally normal now.*

*On October 17, 1986, she was dismissed by her oncologist. His assistant said to us, "I wouldn't even recommend chemotherapy. Just keep on doing what you're presently doing, but I don't want to know what that is!"*

*At the time of this writing, Auntie is in excellent health. She continues to take two teaspoons of [n.n] everyday (and sometimes twice a day if she feels she needs it), along with 3,000-5,000 mg. of vitamin C, a vitamin B complex tablet, one of vitamin E and six alfalfa tablets. The green drink is a daily replacement for our noon meal. We both believe that good nutrition and prayer has saved Auntie's life and will continue to keep both of us physically and spiritually healthy.*

P.S. Auntie's name is Eva Britton. She will celebrate her 100th birthday on December 10, 1998. Judging from her Christmas-card picture, she looks almost as young as I do at 78!  **253, E.B.**

# DIETARY GUIDELINES

## LIST 1
### USDA APPROVED RECOMMENDATIONS*

- **Eat a wider variety of foods in all categories:** A wider variety of vegetables, fruits, whole grains, legumes, meats, nuts, seeds, etc. (We have narrowed our list of favorite foods until we are developing food allergies in epidemic proportions.)
- **Decrease your Intake of "flesh" — beef, pork, fish, poultry, etc.:** Three servings of 3 to 4 oz. each week is all an adult needs for good health. (How much are you eating? Heart disease and many other illnesses could be reduced by obeying this suggestion.)
- **Cut down on foods high In fat and partly substitute polyunsaturated for saturated fats:** (This means less fried foods, ice cream, chips and dips, salad dressings, and a host of our favorite foods. Again, a decrease in cardiovascular disease and obesity could be a benefit of this recommendation.)
- **Cut down on sugar and foods high in sugar:** (Obesity, decayed teeth, cancer, heart disease, kidney stones, candida albicans, diabetes, hypoglycemia, arthritis, and about every illness in the manual is definitely related to our present high sugar consumption. See Chapter V on sugar's effect on our resistance to disease.)
- **Eat more foods that are In the complex carbohydrate category:** (These are vegetables, grains, cereals and beans of all kinds, etc. These foods are good sources of minerals and vitamins and many are significant sources of protein.)
- **Avoid too much salt:** (That's pickles, olives, chips, pork products, salted nuts, and a host of other favorites. Your blood vessels will serve you better if you train yourself to use more herbs as flavorings and less salt in your food.)

*To that should be added: (Author's ideas.)*
- Drink about 2 quarts of water daily (enough to keep your urine pale).
- Exercise 20 minutes three or four times a week at a minimum.
- Eat enough fiber daily so that your bowel movement floats. Oat bran (2 to 3 tablespoons) is a good source of fiber.

*\* Notes in (parentheses) are those of the author.*

## LIST 2

## CARDIOVASCULAR HEALTH LIST

**Eat very sparingly of:**

Regular whole milk,
Evaporated, or condensed milk,
Hard cheeses, regular cottage cheese,
Ice cream and regular yogurt,
Cream and whipped toppings,
Butter, shortening, margarines,
Cream, half & half, lard,
Bacon fat, chocolate, sour cream,
Liver and other organ meats,
Red meats (beef, lamb, pork),
Cold cuts, hotdogs, sausage,
Bacon, egg yolks, spare ribs,
Catfish, herring, mackerel,
Salmon, sardines, swordfish, turbot,
Baked goods (pies, cakes,
cookies, doughnuts, bagels,
Sweet rolls, muffins, white breads),
Sweetened sweet potatoes,
Highly buttered vegetables,
Fried foods,
Batter coated fried foods,
Creamed foods.

**Use these foods more generously:**

Skim or 1% milk, low-fat cheeses/
Low-fat yogurt, farmer or pot cheese,
Ice milk, (if you must!) part-skim milk cheeses,
Buttermilk, tofu,
Dressings, your
own dressings
made with a tomato or yogurt base.
Black bass, bluefish, cod, flounder,
Haddock, perch, pickerel, poultry
(without skin). Water-packed tuna,
Dried beans of all kinds.
Whole-grain breads and cereals
(whole wheat, rye, bran, oatmeal),
Whole-grain rice, whole-wheat spaghetti
Whole wheat noodles,
Whole-wheat pasta of all kinds,
Fresh fruits and vegetables,
Frozen fruits and vegetables,
Canned fruits and vegetables
(Avoid heavy syrup fruits),
Water-packed fruits,
Salt-free vegetables,
Sugar-free vegetables,
Sprouts.

# SUGGESTIONS FOR TAKING GREEN BARLEY

If, after reading this book and being convinced of the attributes of green barley juice, you are ready to try it, then you are about to experience a whole new realm of health and well-being as you join the many users who say, "I wouldn't be without it — I really feel the difference!"

## REMEMBER:

Your green barley powder is bursting with "live" enzymes and co-enzymes (vitamins) that will be destroyed if you "heat" it or freeze it. Therefore:

- DO NOT expose it to sunlight, air, or heat.
- DO NOT mix it with anything hot.
- DO NOT refrigerate it.
- USE ONLY a DRY spoon for getting the powder from the jar.

## FOR BEST RESULTS

- Green barley is taken 30 minutes before or two hours after a meal — always on an empty stomach

- Healthy adults can use daily: 1 to 2 teaspoon servings of green barley powder dissolved in 6 to 8 ounces of water, fruit juice, or milk.

- If you notice detoxification symptoms (see following section on "What to Expect When You Upgrade Your Nutritional Status") it might be best to LOWER your usage for a few days, then go back to a one teaspoon serving and add more gradually.

- If you have a chronic health problem (especially a degenerative disease such as arthritis, cancer, diabetes, or a heart condition, etc.,) many people have reported feeling better by using two teaspoons THREE TIMES A DAY, always observing the guidelines about taking it on an empty stomach.

- Very small children (1-year-olds, for example) often are given 1/4 teaspoon daily, older children 1/2 teaspoon a day, and teenagers one teaspoon or (whatever an adult would take). During times of illness, these amounts may be safely increased for short periods of time, according to Dr. Hagiwara.

- For adults, 20 grams, or about 10 teaspoons daily is considered by Dr. Hagiwara to be the maximum safe number of servings.*

### A WORD OF ADVICE:

Some people find that taking green barley at bedtime causes them to be too energized to sleep well. Others find it a perfect "nightcap" — make sure you have some leeway for experimentation before trying it!

### BE WISE

REMEMBER! If you "feel bad" after starting to take your green barley drink, rejoice! This may very well indicate that your body is initiating the "dump and rebuild" cycle known as detoxification. If you do experience detoxification symptoms, REDUCE YOUR INTAKE for a day or two, but do not stop taking it. Please read the "Detoxification and Cleansing" section in the Appendices.

Last but not least, allow at least 16 to 24 or more weeks to feel the difference. Green barley leaves are not magic, rather, they are an excellent cell food. Given adequate time, dramatic results are frequently reported when directions are carefully and faithfully followed.

*Multitudes of Barley Green users with degenerative disease conditions (i.e., heart disease, cancer, arthritis, diabetes, osteoporosis, etc.) report good to excellent results taking 4-6 teaspoons daily.

# WHAT TO EXPECT WHEN YOU UPGRADE YOUR NUTRITIONAL STATUS

*The ideas presented under this heading are clearly stated in an article entitled, "What Symptoms to Expect When You Improve Your Diet or Improving Your Diet May Make You Sick," by Dr. Stanley S. Bass, D.C. It is very important for first-time green leaves of barley users to understand these concepts. It may very well make the difference between your failure or success in improving your health through better nutrition.*

"When the quality of food that is coming into the body is of higher quality than the tissue which the body is made of, the body begins to discard the lower-grade materials and tissues to make room for the superior materials which it uses to make new and healthier tissue."

At the cellular level, the body is very selective, and continually strives to produce health. (Please see the section on Cell Selection in Chapter IV of this book.) This tendency is inherent in the basic processes of cell metabolism and will always assert itself UNLESS OUR INTERFERENCE IS TOO GREAT! (Too much sugar, too much meat or fat, too many artificial chemicals, too much alcohol consumption, etc., are examples of that.)

What symptoms, then, may surface when we first begin to omit harmful foods and other substances and introduce a superior quality food such as green barley leaves? You can expect your body to get right to work discarding the toxins and the tissues made from the lower quality materials, and replacing it with the higher quality building blocks supplied by the green barley. You may experience one or more of the following, depending on how many changes you are making, what kind of diet you were used to, your medical history, your activity level, your age, and your overall state of health.

When the use of toxic stimulants such as coffee, tea, cocoa or cola is suddenly stopped, headaches are common, and a "letdown" feeling can occur. The cells are discarding such toxins as caffeine, alcohol, nicotine, purines, drugs, preservatives, dead cells, excess bile, fat cells, artery debris, and the like.

Before the noxious substances reach their final destination of elimination, they may be transported through the bloodstream during a number of cycles, causing minor irritation that we interpret as headache pain. Three days will usually see an end to this stage of nutritional improvement.

It is extremely important that we avoid resorting to stimulants or pain killers during this period, as this will defeat the regenerative process going on at the cellular level. Those, who have the patience and persistence to wait it out, will be rewarded by a level of energy and well-being far beyond what can be realized by the use of stimulants or drugs.

Another change that can cause a "let-down" or a sensation of weakness is a decrease in foods from animal flesh. These foods are more stimulating than vegetable proteins. The withdrawal of that source of stimulation can produce a slower heart action, which can register in the mind as relaxation OR as decreased energy. It is important to remember that this initial stage of regeneration usually takes at least 10 days, so that you will not fall prey to discouragement. If you give your body a chance to adjust, you will gain a state of energy that is both higher and has more "staying power."

During the initial stage, the vital energies which are usually invested in the muscles and the skin begin to move to the vital organs as it is required for the work of rebuilding from the inside out. If, for instance, the eliminative organs themselves have been damaged from long abuse, their regeneration and repair will naturally take first priority. Depending on the scope of the needed repair, you can expect a proportionately shorter or longer phase of "rebuilding" or detoxification symptoms.

People who have had tendencies in the past towards skin rashes or eruptions will frequently be those who tend to eliminate poisons and harmful synthetics (like prescription drugs and food preservatives) through the skin. As you upgrade your nutritional status, you may very well see new outbreaks of these rashes or eruptions. This is because the skin is getting more active and alive. It's eliminating poisons more rapidly now, with the energy saved from those hard-to-ingest foods which have been discontinued. Be patient, more perfect skin will almost surely result if you continue to improve the quality of your cell food.

You may even find that colds or fevers which haven't occurred in a long time may recur. This is nature's way of housecleaning. Don't try to stop these symptoms by using drugs, or even massive doses of vitamins (which will act like drugs in heavy concentrations). Toxins are being eliminated that could very well cause you the agony of degenerative disease if they were to remain in your body. Be glad you are dealing with them now on the "easy installment plan," and don't by any means try to cure the cure!

Other symptoms which may occur during detoxification, in addition to the headaches, weakness, "let-down feeling," and skin eruptions we have discussed, include: bowel sluggishness, diarrhea, frequent urination, feelings of tiredness and disinclination to exercise, nervousness, irritability, negativity or mental depression, fevers, and flu-like symptoms. However, the great majority of people find their reactions tolerable and are encouraged to bear with them because of the improvements which are already in evidence and are increasingly obvious with each cycle. (Compare, for instance, the list of symptoms that may occur as side effects of prescription drugs in Appendix F.)

Don't expect that improving your diet will make you feel better and better each day on a linear scale like a ruler. Body processes are cyclical in nature, and health returns in a series of cycles. For example, you start on green barley and a modest program of nutritional upgrades, and for a while you feel much better. After some time, a symptom occurs — you feel nauseous for a day, and have diarrhea with a foul-smelling stool. This passes, and you feel even better than before. All goes fine for awhile, then you suddenly develop a "cold," feel chills and lose your appetite. After about two or three days (assuming you don't take drugs and are able to get extra rest and fluids), you suddenly recover and feel better than you have for years.

As the regeneration process continues, you should find these episodes getting shorter and milder, with longer periods of well-being in between. It's like the stock market in a recovery; every time a reaction occurs, you recover and go a little higher. You may be eating perfectly, taking your green barley and doing all the right things, and still symptoms will occur. These symptoms will vary according to the materials being eliminated, the condition of the organs involved in the elimination, and the amount of energy you have available. The more you rest and sleep when symptoms are present, the milder they will be and the sooner they will end. Be wise, take it easy and relax. Just coast in your work and social obligations until you feel on the upswing again.

You can confidently expect to reach a plateau of vibrant good health, if you persist in using green barley and continue in your progressive campaign to improve your nutritional status.

# DIGESTIVE ENZYME SUPPLEMENTATION

Research has produced evidence that suggests that enzyme supplements are as important to good health as vitamin and mineral supplements. Of course, you know which enzyme supplement I believe is the best — the powdered juice of young barley leaves! But for those with special needs for digestive enzymes, I can make the following suggestions. Digestive enzyme supplementation is especially important to those who:

- Do not include generous quantities of leafy green and yellow vegetables and other raw foods in the daily diet.
- Are elderly and/or under continuous stress.
- Have difficulty with digestion.
- Are suffering from any of the degenerative diseases (heart disease, hypertension, cancer, diabetes, etc.).

Remember! Even having to eat many of your meals at a restaurant or dining hall can be a source of stress to your digestive system. Each food requires its very own set of enzymes. Thus, a typical American salad-bar meal, with small amounts of many different foods, is actually a stress situation for the body!

There are a number of good products available. Taken according to directions, they work much like digestive enzymes made by the body. In shopping for a digestive enzyme supplement, read labels carefully. Unless you know your exact needs from clinical testing, it seems logical to buy a broad spectrum product that aids in digesting proteins, fats and carbohydrates.

Full-spectrum digestive-aid tablets often contain enzymes which work in the stomach or the duodenum. Enzymes which work in the stomach are: betaine hydrochloric acid, glutamic acid, HC1, pepsin, and papain. Enzymes which work in the duodenum are: pancreatin, pancrelipase, amylase, bromelain, and many include an animal bile extract. Once opened, these products should be kept in a dark, cool, dry place! (Phone us for product recommendations.)

# DIETARY GUIDELINES TO LOWER CANCER RISK*

## FRUIT AND VEGETABLE GROUP:

**Liberal Consumption:**

- Dark-green leafy vegetables (kale, collards, turnip greens, spinach, chard, mustard greens)
- Deep yellow vegetables (sweet potatoes, squashes, carrots), apricots, peaches, cantaloupe
- Vitamin C rich fruits & vegetables (citrus fruits, cabbage, tomatoes, watermelon, strawberries, spinach, broccoli, brussels sprouts)

## PROTEIN GROUPS:

**Liberal Consumption:**

- Legumes (Dried beans and peas of all kinds)

**Moderate Consumption:**

- Lean beef, fish, poultry, lamb
- Low-fat milk, low-fat yogurt, low-fat cheese (American, cottage, Swiss, skim-milk cheeses)

**Very Moderate Consumption:**

- Fatty meats, sausage, salt-cured, smoked and charcoal broiled foods
- Whole milk, cheese, nuts, seeds, eggs

## GRAIN GROUP:

**Liberal Consumption:**

- Whole grains (rice, oats, wheat, barley, millet, rye, etc.)
- Whole grain cereals

## EMPTY CALORIE GROUP:

**Sparse Consumption:**

- Rich desserts, soft drinks, alcohol, fats, oils, chips, candy, jams & jellies, cookies, doughnuts and salty foods

*[Examples of specific foods in each category, by the author.]*

*"Both saturated and unsaturated dietary fats have been linked to cancers, particularly breast, prostate and colon cancers. The National Academy of Sciences recommends that the consumption of both saturated fats (animal origin) and unsaturated fats (plant origin, e.g., corn oil, safflower oil) be reduced in the average U.S. diet."*

*"The data is clear THE AMOUNT OF FAT is the overriding factor. The type of fat also makes a difference but . . . the total number of (fat) calories consumed may be even more important."*

*"Unsaturated fats (the oils) tend to increase tumor development more than saturated fats (animal fat) in most studies. Unsaturated fats (the oils) tend to lower the risk of heart disease. Do we have to trade risk of heart disease in order to lower risk of cancer? According to Dr. Campbell, professor of nutrition at Cornell University, "I believe we can do both by decreasing total fat in our diets — by eating less fried foods, spreads and oils while eating more plant products."*

*"One recommendation I am enthusiastic about because of the scientific base is to eat more fruits, vegetables and whole grain products — shift to a more plant-oriented diet. This type of diet would meet both the guidelines for heart disease and for cancer. It would reduce total fat and protein intake and increase dietary fiber, beta-carotene and ascorbic acid intake."*

*Prepared by: Dr. Mary Ruth Swope, Swope Enterprises, Inc., Taken from the Fall 1984 Newsletter, American Institute of Cancer Research, Washington DC.

# Side Effects of Commonly Prescribed Drugs

| SIDE EFFECTS | Antacids | Anti-Arthritic | Anti-Asthmatic | Antibiotic | Anti-Clotting | Anti-Coagulants | Anti-Depressants | Anti-Diabetic | Antihistamine | Anti-Inflammatory | Anti-Virus | Appetite Suppressants | Blood Pressure Pills | Blood Thinners | Blood Vessel Dialtors | Diuretics (Water Pills) | Female Hormones | Muscle Relaxers | Phlegm Looseners | Sedatives (pain) | Sleeping Aids | Tranquilizers | Vasodilators |
|---|---|---|---|---|---|---|---|---|---|---|---|---|---|---|---|---|---|---|---|---|---|---|---|
| Abdominal Pain | | • | | • | • | | | | | | | | | | | | | | | • | | | |
| Angina Pain | | • | | | | | | | | | | | | | | | | | | | | | |
| Anorexia | | • | | | | | | | | | | | | | | | | | | | | | |
| Anxiety | | • | | | | | | • | | | | | | | | | | | | | | | |
| Arrythmia | | • | | | | • | | | | | | | | | | | | | | | | | |
| Bleeding | | | | | | | | | | | | | | | | | • | | | | | | |
| Bloated Feeling | • | | | | | | | | | | | | | | | | | | | | | | |
| Blood Sugar problems | | | | | | | | • | | | | | | | | | | • | | | | | |
| Blurred vision | | | | | | | • | | | | | | | | | • | | • | | | | | • |
| Breast Enlargement | | | | | | | • | | | | | | | | | | • | • | | | | | |
| Chills | | | • | | | | | • | | | | | | | | | | | | | | | |
| Cold sweats | | | | | | | • | | | | | | | | | | | | | | | | |
| Confusion | | | | | | | • | | | | | • | | | | | | • | | • | | • | |
| Constipation | • | • | • | | • | | | | | | | • | • | • | | | | | | • | • | | |

| SIDE EFFECTS | Antacids | Anti-Arthritic | Anti-Asthmatic | Antibiotic | Anti-Clotting | Anti-Coagulants | Anti-Depressants | Anti-Diabetic | Antihistamine | Anti-Inflammatory | Anti-Virus | Appetite Suppressants | Blood Pressure Pills | Blood Thinners | Blood Vessel Dilators | Diuretics (Water Pills) | Female Hormones | Muslce Relaxers | Phlegm Looseners | Sedatives (pain) | Sleeping Aids | Tranquilizers | Vasodilators |
|---|---|---|---|---|---|---|---|---|---|---|---|---|---|---|---|---|---|---|---|---|---|---|---|
| Decreased Growth (child) | | | | | | | | | | | | | | | | | | | | | | | |
| Decreased Resistance to infection | | | | | | | | | | | | ● | ● | | | | | | | | | | |
| Depression | | | | | | | ● | | | | | ● | ● | | | | | ● | | | | ● | |
| Diarrhea | ● | ● | ● | ● | ● | | | | | | | | ● | | | ● | | | | | | ● | |
| Dizziness | | ● | ● | ● | ● | ● | ● | ● | ● | ● | ● | | ● | ● | | ● | ● | ● | ● | | | ● | ● |
| Drowsiness | | ● | ● | ● | | ● | ● | ● | ● | | | | | | | | | ● | ● | ● | ● | ● | |
| Dry mouth/throat | | | ● | | | ● | ● | ● | | | | | ● | ● | | ● | ● | ● | | | ● | | |
| Fatigue | | ● | ● | | | | ● | | | | | | | | | | | | | | ● | | |
| Fear | | ● | | ● | | | | | | | | | ● | | | | | | | | ● | | |
| Fever | | | ● | | | | | | | | | | | | | | | | | | | | |
| Fluid retention | ● | | | | | | ● | | | ● | | | | | | | ● | | | | | | ● |
| Flushing | | | ● | | | ● | | | | | | | ● | ● | | | | | | | | ● | ● |
| Glaucoma | | ● | | | | | | | | ● | | | | | | | | | | | | | |
| Hallucinations | | | | | | ● | | | | | | | | | | | | | | | | | |
| Headaches | | ● | ● | ● | | | ● | ● | ● | ● | | | ● | ● | | ● | | ● | | ● | ● | ● | ● |
| Heart Disease | ● | ● | | | | ● | | | | | | | | | | | ● | | | | | | |
| High blood pressure | ● | ● | | | | ● | | | | | ● | | | | | | | | | | | | |
| Hives | | | | ● | | | | | | | | | | | | | | | | | | | |
| Impaired coordination | | ● | | | | | ● | ● | | | | | | ● | | | | | | | | | ● |
| Insomnia | | ● | | | | | ● | ● | | | | | | | | | | | | | | | |
| Irritability | | ● | | | | | ● | | | | ● | | | | | | | | | | | | |
| Itching | | ● | | | ● | ● | | ● | | | ● | ● | | | | ● | | | | ● | | | ● |
| Jaundice | | | | | | ● | ● | | | | | | | | | | | | ● | ● | | ● | |
| Kidney damage | ● | ● | | | | | | | | | | | | | | | | | | | | | |
| Liver damage | | | | | | | | | | | | | | | | | | | | | ● | ● | |
| Loss of Appetite | | | | ● | | | ● | | | | | ● | ● | | | | | ● | | | | | |

| SIDE EFFECTS | Antacids | Anti-Arthritic | Anti-Asthmatic | Antibiotic | Anti-Clotting | Anti-Coagluants | Anti-Depressants | Anti-Diabetic | Antihistamine | Anti-Inflammatory | Anti-Virus | Anppetite Suppressants | Blood Pressure Pills | Blood Thinners | Blood Vessel Diators | Diuretics (Water Pills) | Female Hormones | Muslce Relaxers | Phlegm Looseners | Sedatives (pain) | Sleeping Aids | Tranquilizers | Vasodilators |
|---|---|---|---|---|---|---|---|---|---|---|---|---|---|---|---|---|---|---|---|---|---|---|---|
| Lowered Blood Pressure | | | • | | | | • | | | | | | • | | | | • | | | • | | • | • |
| Mental confusion | | | | | | | • | | | | | | | | | | | | | | | | |
| Menstrual problems | | | | | | | • | | • | | | | | | | | • | | | | | | |
| Mood swings | | | | | | | • | | | | | | | | | | | | | | | | |
| Muscle cramps | • | | • | | | | | | | | | | | | | | • | • | | | | | |
| Muscle weakness | | | | | | | • | | | | | | | | | | | | | | | | |
| Nausea | • | | • | • | | | • | • | | | • | | • | | | • | | • | • | • | • | • | |
| Numbness | | | | | | | | | | • | | | | | | | | | | | | | |
| Psychosis | | | | | | | | | | | | • | | | | | | | | | | | |
| Rapid heartbeat | • | | | | | • | | | | | | • | | | | | | | • | | | | • |
| Restlessness | | | • | | | | | | | | | • | | | | • | | | | | | | |
| Ringing ears | • | | | | | • | | | | | | | | | | | | | | | | | |
| Sex impotence | | | | | | | • | | | | • | | | | | | | | | | | | |
| Skin rash | • | • | • | • | • | • | • | | | | | | • | | | • | | • | | • | • | • | |
| Sleepiness | | • | | | | | | | | | | | | | | | | | | | | | |
| Sleeplessness | | | | | | | • | | • | • | | | | | | | • | | | | • | | |
| Slow healing | | | | | | | | • | | | | | | | | | | | | | | | |
| Sweating | • | | | | | | • | | | | | | | | | | | | | • | | | |
| Tension | • | | | | | | | | | | | | | | | | | | | | | | |
| Tightness in chest | • | | | | | | | | | | | | | | | | | | | | | | |
| Tingling feeling | | | | | | | • | | | | | | | | | | • | | | | | | |
| Tiredness | • | | • | | | • | • | | • | | | | | • | • | | | • | • | | • | | |
| Trembling | | | • | | | | • | | • | | | | | • | • | | | | | | | | |
| Upset stomach | | • | • | • | | | | | | • | | | | | | | • | | | | | | |
| Ulcers | | • | | | | | | | | • | | | | | | • | | | | | | • | • |
| Vomiting | • | • | • | • | | | | | • | • | | | | • | | | • | | | | • | | |
| Weakness | | | | | | | • | • | | | | | | | | | | • | • | | • | | |

# BIBLIOGRAPHY AND FOOTNOTES

## CHAPTER 1

1. Black, Dean, Ph.D., *Health at the Crossroads*, Tapestry Press, 1988, p. 3.
2. Atkins, Robert C., M.D., *Dr. Atkins Health Revolution*, Houghton Mifflin Company, Boston, Mass. 1988, pp. 42-43.
3. Hippocrates: Castiglioni, A., *A History of Medicine*, New York: Alfred A. Knops, 1958, p. 172.
4. Rush, Benjamin, Sixteen Introduction Lectures to Courses of Lectures upon the Institutes and Practice of Medicine, delivered at the University of Pennsylvania (Philadelphia: Bradford & Innskeep,1811) p. 165.
5. Coulter, Harris L., *Divided Legacy: A History of the Schism in Medical Thought*, Vol. III Washington, D.C.: McGrath, 1973) p. 90.
6. *Proceeding of the Connecticut Medical Society for 1850.* Bound pamphlets printed in Norwich & Hartford, Vol. 1244, p. 53.
7. Atkins, op.cit., p. 26.
8. Ibid. pp. 26-27.
9. *Physicians' Desk Reference*, 27th Edition, Medical Economics Company, Oradell, N.J., 1973, p. 593.
10. Black op.cit., p. 14.
11. Ibid. p. 21.
12. The impact of Nutrition On the Health of Americans, The Bard College Center, Annandale-on-Hudson, New York, *The Medicine & Nutrition Project*, Report No.1, The Ford Foundation, July,1981, p. II/23.
13. Black, op.cit., p. 71.
14. Ibid. p. 4.
15. Atkins, op.cit., p. 59.
16. Ibid. pp. 9-10.
17. Ibid. p. 50.
18. Ibid. p. 48.

## CHAPTER 2

1. Yoshihide Hagiwara, M.D., *Green Barley Essence*, Keats Publishing, Inc., New Canaan, 1985 pp. 9-10.
2. *Statistical Abstract of the U.S., U.S. Department of Commerce Bureau of the Census*, 1995, Chart 225, p. 147.

3.   *The Book of Health Secrets,* Boardman Classics, N.Y., N.Y. 1989 p. 147.
4.   Dean Black, Ph D., *Health at the Crossroads*, Tapestry Press, Springville, Utah, p. 49.
5.   Brent O. Hafen, *Nutrition, Food and Weight Control*, Allyn and Bacon, Inc., Boston, 1981, p. 125. 4. FDA Special Report, op.cit., p. 5.
6.   Sang Whand, *"Reverse Aging not Science Fiction But Scientific Fact."* Copyright 1990 by author, Miami, FL.
7.   Francisco Contraras, M.D., Speech given at American Image Marketing Convention, 1990; taken from an audio tape.
8.   Journal of Clinical Epidemiology, Vol. 45, 911, 1992.
9.   FDA Consumer, October 1980, p. 7.
10.  FDA Consumer, October 1980, p. 9.
11.  Taken from an article entitled, *"Confessions of a Soft Drink."* Regretfully the exact author and publisher have been misplaced, p. 10.
12.  Earl Mindell, *"Unsafe At Any Meal,"* Warner Books, N.Y. 1987, p. 119.
13.  Ibid.

## CHAPTER 3

1.   Merrill *Unger's Bible Dictionary*, Moody Press, Chicago, 1977, p. 1134.
2.   *World Book Encyclopedia*, Vol. 2, 1986, p. 80.
3.   Funk & Wagnalls, *New Encyclopedia*, Vol. 3, 1986, p. 282.
4.   Joseph Kadans, *Encyclopedia of Fruits, Vegetables, Nuts, and Seeds for Healthful Living*, Parker Publishing Co., Inc., W. Nyack, 1973, p. 73.
5.   Nelson Coons, *Using Plants in Healing*, Rodale Press, Emmaus, 1963, p. 227.
6.   Dr. Bernard Jensen, *Foods that Heal*, Avery Publishing Group, Inc., Garden City Park, NY, 1988, p. 9.
7.   Yoshihide Hagiwara, M.D., *Green Barley Essence*, Keats Publishing Co., New Canaan, 1985, p. XXVII.
8.   John D. Kirschmann and Lavon Dunne, *Nutrition Almanac*, McGraw-Hill Book Company, New York, 2nd Ed., 1984, p. 235.
9.   Wesley Marx, *Seaweed, the Ocean's Unsung Gift,* Reader's Digest, Vol. 124, No. 746, Jun. 1984, p. 48.
10.  Peter Bradford and Montse Bradford, *Cooking With Sea Vegetables*, Thorson's Publishing Group, Wellingborough, 1985, p. 60.
11.  Kirschmann and Dunne, op. cit., p. 251.

## CHAPTER 4

1.   William P. Pinkston, Jr., *Biology*, Bob Jones University Press, Greenville, 1980, p. 71.
2.   Ibid.
3.   Arthur Guyton, *Textbook of Medical Physiology*, W. B. Saunders Co., Philadelphia, 1981, p. 12.

4.  Ibid. p. 13.
5.  Pinkston, op.cit., p. 73.
6.  Ibid. p. 897.
7.  Guyton, op.cit., pp. 896-898.
8.  Pinkston, op.cit., p. 668.
9.  Guyton, op.cit., p. 12.
10. Ibid. p. 2.
11. Hans Selye, M.D., *The Stress of Life*, McGraw-Hill, NY, 1978, pp. xi-xvii.
12. Guyton, op.cit., p. 370.
13. Lawrence Lauch, M.D., *Metabolics*, 1974, p. 9.

## CHAPTER 5

1.  Bruce Harstead, "Immune Augmentation Therapy," *Journal of the International Academy of Preventive Medicine*, Vol. 9, No. 1, Aug. 1985, p. 5.
2.  National Institute of Health, *Understanding the Immune System*, U.S. Dept. of Health and Human Services, NIH Publication 85-529, reprinted July 1985, p. 2.
3.  Ibid, p. 4.
4.  Halstead, p. 9.
5.  Jaret, Peter, "Our Immune System: The Wars Within," *National Geographic Magazine*, Vol. 169, No. 6, June 1986, p. 706.
6.  NIH, p.6.
7.  Weiner, Michael A., Ph.D., *Maximum Immunity*, Pocket Books, New York, 1986, pp. 21-22.
8.  NIH, p. 4.
9.  Weiner, pp. 22-23.
10. *World Book Encyclopedia*.
11. Weiner, p. 22.
12. Ibid, p. 30.
13. Agatha Thrash, M.D., *Lecture Notes*, Uchee Pines Institute, Seal, AL. 1983.
14. Weiner, p. 82.
15. Ibid, p. 85.
16. Ibid, p. 86.
17. Ibid, p. 86.
18. Ibid, p. 108.
19. Ibid, pp. 108-109.
20. William Beisel, et al "Single-Nutrient Effects on Immunologic Function," *Journal of American Medical Association*, Vol. 245, No. 1, Jan. 2, 1981, p. 55.
21. Weiner, p. 111.
22. Ibid.
23. Ibid, p. 112.
24. JAMA, p. 55.
25. Ibid.
26. Weiner, p. 114.

27. JAMA, p. 55.
28. Weiner, p. 117.
29. Ibid, p. 121.
30. Ibid. p. 122.
31. JAMA, p. 56.
32. Weiner, p. 127.
33. Ibid.

## CHAPTER 6

1. G.A. Hendry and O.T. Jones, "Haems and Chlorophylls: Comparisons of Function & Formation," *Journal of Medical Genetics* 1980, Feb. 17 (1 ) p. 1.
2. Lois Mattox Miller, "Chlorophyll for Healing," *Science News Letter* March 15, 1941, p. 170.
3. Paul de Kruif, "Nature's Deodorant," *Reader's Digest*, Aug. 1950, Vol. 57, p. 139.
4. Ibid
5. Ibid.
6. "Is Chlorophyll All the Admen Say?" *Business Week* April 1952, Vol. 165, p. 165.
7. J. Jancy, "Lack of Sobering Effect of Fructose-Vitamin Tablets," *Medical Journal of Australia,* March 28, 1970, 1 (13) p. 688.
8. *New Republic,* Nov. 10, 1952, p. 8.
9. Leonard Engel, "Can Chlorophyll Stop 'B.O.' ?" *Science Digest*, October 1952, Vol. 32, p. 36.
10. Engel, pp. 37-38.
11. "Chlorophyll," *Consumer Report* October 1952, Vol. 17, pp. 488-89.
12. Engel, p. 37.
13. de Kruif, pp. 141-142.
14. "Chlorophyll Compounds Show Heart-Aid Action," *Science News Letter,* October 11, 1958, p. 233.
15. Dr. J.A. Driskell, Professor and Head, Department of Human Nutrition and Foods, Virginia Polytechnic Institute and State University.
16. Lawrence W. Smith, "The Present Status of Topical Chlorophyll Therapy," *New York State Journal of Medicine*, July 15, Vol. 55, p. 2041.
17. *Science News Letter*, Oct. 11, 1958, p. 233.
18. Miller, p. 170.
19. Ibid, p. 170.
20. Hendry and Jones, p. 14.
21. Benjamin Gruskin, "Chlorophyll Its Therapeutic Place in Acute and Suppurative Diseases," *American Journal of Surgery*, July 1940, p. 50.
22. Paul Sack and Robert Barnard, "Studies on Hemagglutinating and Inflammatory Properties of Exudate from Nonhealing Wounds & Their

Inhibition by Chlorophyll Derivatives," *New York State Journal of Medicine*, Oct. 15, 1955, Vol. 55, p. 2952.

23. Ibid pp. 2955.
24. Gruskin, p. 54.
25. Ibid, p. 54.
26. Smith, pp. 20-43.
27. Engel, p. 39.
28. Smith, pp. 20-44.
29. Ibid, pp. 20-45.
30. de Kruif, pp. 139-140.
31. Smith, p. 2044.
32. L.H. Siegel, "The Control of Ileostomy and Colostomy Odors," *Gastroenterology*, Apr. 1960, Vol. 38, pp. 635-636.
33. Richard Young & Joseph Beregi, "Use of Chlorophyllin in Care of Geriatric Patients," *American Geriatrics Society Journal*, Jan. 1980, Vol. 28, No. 1, p. 47.
34. Milap Nahatal et al, "Effect of Chlorophyllin on Urinary Odor in Incontinent Geriatric Patients," *Drug Intelligence & Clinical Pharmacy*, Oct. 1983, Vol. 17, p. 734.
35. H.E. Averette, "Lymphography With Chlorophyll: Effects on Pelvic Lymphadenectomy with Lymph Nodes," *Obstetrics's Gynecology*, Feb. 1968, Vol. 31, p. 253.
36. Theodore Wiznitzer, et al, "Acute Necrotizing Pancreatitis in the Guinea Pig: Effect of Chlorophyll-a on Survival Times," *Digestive Diseases*, June 1976, Vol. 21, No. 6, p. 459.
37. S.K. Mann and N.S. Mann, "Effect of Chlorophyll-a, Flurouracil, and Pituitrin on Experimental Acute Pancreatitis," *Archives of Pathological Laboratory Medicine*, Feb. 1979, Vol. 103.
38. Tadeo Manabe, Michael Steer, "Protease Inhibitors and Experimental Acute Hemorrhagic Pancreatitis," *Annals of Surgery*, July 1979, Vol. 190. No. 1, pp. 13-14.
39. R. Tawashi, et al, "Effect of Sodium Copper Chlorophyllin on the Formation of Calcium Oxalate Crystals in Rat Kidney," *Investigative Urology*, Sept. 1980, Vol. 18, No. 2, p. 90.
40. R. Tawashi and M. Cousineau, "Growth Retardation of Weddellite (Calcium Oxalate Dihydrate) by Sodium Copper Chlorophyllin," *Investigative Urology*, Sept. 1980, Vol. 18, No. 2, pp. 86-89.
41. R. Tawashi, et al, "Crystallization of Calcium Oxalate Dihydrate in Normal Urine in Presence of Sodium Copper Chlorophyllin," *Urological Research* 1982, Vol. 10, No. 4, p. 173.

## CHAPTER 7

1. Arthur C. Guyton, M.D. *Textbook of Medical Physiology*, W.B. Saunders Co., Philadelphia, 1981, pp. 448-450.
2. Rubard Leek, PH.D., "Acidosis and Alkalosis: Symptoms and Treatments," *The Nutrition and Dietary Consultant*, Oct. 1985.
3. Margaret Justin, et all, *Foods*, Houghton Mifflin Co., Boston, 4th Ed., pp.42-43.
4. Ibid, p. 26.
5. Margaret Chaney and Margaret Ross, *Nutrition*, Houghton Mifflin Co., Boston, 7th Ed., p. 326.
6. Agatha Thrash, M.D., *Eat for Strength Not For Drunkenness*, Uchee Pines Institute, Seale, AL. p. 182.
7. Leek, op.cit., p. 14.
8. Robert H. Garrison, Jr., *The Nutrition Desk Reference*, Keats Publishing Co., New Canaan, 1985, p. 106.
9. Ibid.
10. Ibid.
11. Ibid.
12. Ibid.
13. Leek, op. cit., p. 15.

## CHAPTER 8

1. Howell, Edward, *Enzyme Nutrition*, Avery Publishing Group, Inc., Wayne, NJ, 1985.
2. Howell, Edward, *The Status of Food Enzymes in Digestion and Metabolism*, (Chicago: National Enzyme Co., 1946), p. 72
3. Howell, op-cit, p. XI.
4. Ibid, p. 29.
5. Ibid, p. 107
6. Howell, Edward, *Enzyme Nutrition*, Avery Publishing Group, Inc., Wayne, NJ, 1985.
7. Ibid, p. 109
8. Ibid, p. 112.
9. Ibid, p. 43.
10. Ibid, p. 50.
11. William Campbell Douglas, M.D., *The Milk of Human Kindness*, Last Laugh Publishers, Marietta, Ga., 1985, pp. 42-43.

## CHAPTER 9

1. Yoshihide Hagiwara, M.D., *Green Barley Essence*, Keats Publishing Co., New Canaan, 1985, p. 73.
2. Robert Picher, M.D., *Barley Green: Guardian Against Cancer*, The Center for Holistic and Nutritional Medicine, Berkeley, 1985.
3. Yoshihide Hagiwara, M.D., "Prevention of Aging and Adult Diseases and

Methods of Longevity and Good Health," an abstract, lecture given at Pacific Beach Hotel, Honolulu, April 13, 1984, p. 5.

4. Kazuhiko Kubota, Ph.D., "Scientific Investigations on Young Barley Juice Powder," Lecture given at Pacific Beach Hotel, Honolulu, April 13,1984, p. I.

5. Hagiwara, lecture, op. cit., p. 6.

6. *Nutrition News*, September, 1982.

7. Hagiwara, *Green Barley Essence*, op. cit., p. 136.

8. Kubota, Ph.D., op. cit. p. 1.

9. Yasuo Hotta, DS., "Stimulation of DNA Repair Synthesis by $P_4D_1$, One of the Novel Components of Barley Extracts," lecture, Pacific Beach Hotel, Honolulu 4/13/84.

10. Ibid.

11. Ibid.

12. Ibid.

13. Ibid.

14. Hagiwara, *Green Barley Essence* op. cit., p. 137.

15. Ibid.

16. Jeffrey Blands Ph.D. (ed), 1984-85 *Yearbook of Nutritional Medicine*, Keats Publishing Co., New Canaan, 1985 p. 168.

17. Irwin Fridovich, "The Biology of Superoxide and of Superoxide Dismutases - in Brief," *Progress in Clinical and Biological Research*, Vol. 51, 1981, pp. 154-155.

18. Ibid, p. 159.

19. Joe M. McCord, "Free Radicals and Inflammation: Protection of Synovial Fluid by Superoxide Dismutase," *Science*, Vol. 185, Aug. 1974, pp. 529-530.

20. Robert J. Boucek, M.D., "Factors Affecting Wound Healing," *Otobryngologic Clinics of North America*, Vol. 17, No. 2, May 1984, p. 244.

21. Irwin Fridovich, "Superoxide Dismutases: Regularities and Irregularities," Lecture delivered November 17, 1983, The Harvey Lectures, Series 79, Academic Press, Inc., 1985, pp. 64-65.

22. Myron Weisfeldt, Johns Hopkins School of Medicine, *Science*, Vol. 232, Jun. 6, 1986, p. 1198.

23. Charles Puglia and Saul Powell, "Inhibition of Cellular Antioxidants: A Possible Mechanism of Toxic Cell Injury," *Environmental Health Perspectives*, Vol. 57, 1987, pp. 307-311.

24. Fridovich, Harvey, Lectures, op. cit., p. 63.

25. Editor, "Supergene Cluster Fights Aging," *Science Digest*, Vol. 90, Aug. 1982, p. 91.

26. Thomas Kensler, et.al., "Inhibition of Tumor Promotion by a Biomimetic Superoxide Dismutase," *Science*, Vol. 231, Jul. 1, 1983, pp. 75-77.

## CHAPTER 10

1. Adrianne Bendich, Carotenoids and the Immune Response, *Journal of Nutrition*, 119:112-115, 1989.
2. Ibid.
3. *Science News*, Vol. 135, June 3, 1989, p. 348.
4. Hagiwara, op cit., p. 80.
5. Ibid., p. 58.

## CHAPTER 11

1. Tatsuo Muto, "Therapeutic Experiment of Bakuryokuso (young barley juice) for the Treatment of Skin Diseases in Man," *New Drugs and Clinical Application*, Vol. 26, No. 5, May 10, 1977.
2. Kazuhiko Kubota and Nubuyoshi Sunagane, *"Studies of the Effects of Green Barley Juice on the Endurance and Motor Activity in Mice,"* Faculty of Pharmaceutical Sciences, Science University of Tokyo, Tokyo, 162 Japan.
3. Ibid.
4. Kazuhiko Kubota, Yutaka Matsuoka, *"Effect of Chronic Administration of Green Barley Juice on Growth Rate, Serum Cholesterol Level and Internal Organs of Mice,"* Faculty of Pharmaceutical Sciences, Science University of Tokyo, 12, Tokyo, 162, Japan.
5. Ibid.
6. *"Isolation of Potent Anti-Inflammatory Protein From Barley Leaves,"* Faculty of Pharmaceutical Sciences, Science University of Tokyo, 162, Japan.
7. Hiditoshi Ohtake, Hideo Yuasa, Chiseko Komura, Tetsuji Miyauchi, Yoshihide Hagiwara, Kazuhiko Kubota, *"Anti-ulcer Activity of Fractions From Barley Juice,"* Research Laboratory, Japan Pharmaceutical Development Co., LTD, 1-1-26, Mitsuya Minami, Yodogawaku, Osaka, 532, Japan.
8. *Journal of Nutritional Biochemistry*, Vol. 5, March 1994, pp. 145-150.
9. T. Nishlyama, Y. Hagiwara, H. Hagiwara, and T. Shibamoto, *"Inhibition of Malonaldehyde Formation from Lipids by an Isoflavonoid Isolated from Young Green Barley Leaves,"* Department of Environmental Toxicology, University of California, Davis, California 95616.
10. Osamu Yokono, M.D., *"Therapeutic Effect of Water-Soluble Form of Chlorophyll-A and the Related Substance of Young Barley Green Juice in the Treatment of Patients with Chronic Pancreatitis,"* Faculty of Medicine. University of Tokyo, Tokyo, Japan.
11. T. Shibamoto, Y. Hagiwara, H. Hagiwara, T. Osawa, "Flavonoid with Strong Antioxidative Activity Isolated From Young Barley Leaves," *Food Phytochemicals II: Teas, Spices, and Herbs, American Chemical Society*, Chapter 17, 1994, p. 154.
12. Ibid, p. 161

## POSTSCRIPT ONE

As this book was on the printing press and ready to roll, I attended a conference in which the results of a very exciting double-blind study were reported.

Dr. Eugene Wagner, a professor of medical biochemistry at the Indiana University School of Medicine at Ball State University in Muncie, Indiana, was the chief researcher.

Sparked by a personal experience with green barley products, he set out to determine whether or not it could rightfully be said that such food products strengthen the immune system.

Thirty-two students participated in the study. They were randomly divided into two groups of 16. One group received three teaspoons of a popular barley product each day. The control group received green-colored rice powder.

After 71 days, blood from each participant was drawn and a CBC differential count was made and compared with their initial blood workups. The comparison showed that among the barley-taking students, two components of the first line of defense in the immune system, the neutrophils and complement, were statistically significantly different that of the control group. These components were strengthened within the normal range.

From this it could be hypothesized that, indeed, the immune systems' first line of defense in the barley students was stronger than at the outset of the study. This could also explain another important fact. Only two of the 16 suffered upper respiratory ailments during the period, whereas 10 of the 16 in the control group suffered similar respiratory distress.

# POSTSCRIPT TWO

Postscript one was written in 1994. and now, in 1996, as this printing is ready to roll, I have something new to add that is exciting to me.

Years of study and experience have fully confirmed that Nature has provided a wide variety of delicious and nutritious foods perfectly designed for the growth maintenance and repair of all tissue. This truth was magnified exponentially to me as I recently read and understood results of years of the research by a number of botanists from various countries of the world.

Beginning in the later part of the 19th century, and continuing until today scientific investigations by the hundreds, in different fields, have shown us undeniably that everything in the universe radiates electromagnetic waves which can be identified as sound, color, form, movement, perfume, temperature and "innate awareness."

While all plant radiations differ from one another (like our thumb prints and snow flakes!) they have a time when the radiations are at their peak. In most cases this coincides with the height of their maturity, which is also near a full moon.

Now buckle your seatbelts and trust me. What I want to share is purely scientific evidence but it validates perfectly the account in Genesis 1:29. God told Adam and Eve, "Behold I have given you every plant yielding seed that is on the surface of all the earth and every tree which has fruit yielding seed; for you this is meat."

A botanist from France developed an instrument called a biometer which enabled him to measure frequencies being emitted from foods, in centimeters and angstroms*.

The wavelengths coming from the foods could tell both their freshness and the vitality or strength of the food.

---

* An angstrom is 100 millionth of a centimeter - a unit in measuring the length of light waves.

Now for the part that is thrilling to me. Without exception, the foods with the highest number of angstroms are the foods God told Adam and Eve to eat. Here is the list:

**10,000 to 8,500 angstroms** — Barley, wheat, oats and other grains; butter and garlic; fruits and vegetables if eaten fresh; olive oil; and legumes, lentils and beans.

**6,500 down to 3,000 angstroms** — fresh milk, wine, peanut oil, boiled fruits and vegetables, unrefined cane sugar, canned fish and dried foods.

**No angstrom foods** — coffee, tea, chocolate, jams, cheeses, white bread, day-old milk, margarines, jellies, canned fruits, canned vegetables, alcohols, liquors, white sugar, bleached white four, pasteurized fruit and vegetable juices.

Space does not permit more about food angstroms in this edition. But please, accept the facts whether or not you fully understand the science behind them.

**We _were_ designed to thrive on raw fruits, vegetables, grains, nuts, seeds, berries, and the beans, legumes and lentils. These are the foods that energize our bodies, build strong immune systems, heal us when we are sick and make us radiantly healthy.**

Gamble on it! What do you have to lose?

# INDEX

## BOOKS BY DR. MARY RUTH SWOPE

| | |
|---|---|
| Green Leaves of Barley: Nature's Miracle Rejuvenator - Updated Edition  *New '96* | $ 9.95 |
| *Other translations available* | |
| Surviving The 20th Century Diet: Scientific Solutions To A Diet Gone Wrong | $ 6.95 |
| *New for '96 - The Abridged Version of Green Leaves of Barley* | |
| Some Gold Nuggets in Nutrition - *Enlarged and Updated for '96* | $ 4.00 |
| The Roots and Fruits of Fasting   *New '98* | $ 6.00 |
| The Spiritual Roots of Barley | $ 5.00 |
| Lifelong Health | $ 6.00 |
| Listening Prayer | $ 5.00 |
| Fasting...Physical & Spiritual Benefits | $ 1.00 |
| Bless Your Children Every Day | $ 9.95 |

## OTHER RECOMMENDED BOOKS

| | |
|---|---|
| What Your Doctor May Not Tell You About Menopause by John R. Lee, M.D. | $13.00 |
| Green Barley Essence by Dr. Yoshihide Hagiwara     (Abridged version available) | $10.95 |
| Health in the 21st Century by Francisco Contreras, M.D. | $18.00 |
| God's Way To Ultimate Health by Rev. George H. Malkmus | $18.95 |
| Why Christians Get Sick by Rev. George H. Malkmus | $ 8.95 |
| Recipes for Life from God's Garden by Rhonda J. Malkmus | $24.95 |
| Country Life Vegetarian Cookbook edited by Diana J. Fleming | $ 9.95 |
| Ten Talents Cookbook by Frank J. Hurd, D.C., M.D. and Rosalie Hurd, B.S. | $21.95 |
| Antioxidants, Coenzyme Q10, Ginko Biloba by Dr. E. S. Wagner, Ph.D. (each $1.00) or "Trio" | $ 2.95 |
| Fasting and Eating for Health by Joel Fuhrman, M.D. | $24.95 |
| Cleansing the Body & The Colon by Teresa Schumacher and Toni S. Lund | $ 3.95 |
| Of These Ye May Freely Eat by Jeani McKeever | $ 3.95 |

## AUDIO CASSETTE TAPES BY DR. SWOPE

| | | |
|---|---|---|
| Newer Concepts in Nutrition  *New in '98* | (Two Tape Set) | $ 8.00 |
| The New Health Model  *New in '98* | (Two Tape Set) | $ 8.00 |
| Use Blessings Everyday | (1 Tape) | $ 3.00 |
| Understanding The Family of Plants and Research: The Foundation Stone  *New in '96* | | $ 4.00 |

## VIDEO TAPES

| | | |
|---|---|---|
| Nutrition Update...BarleyGreen by Swope/Darbro | (30 minutes) | $16.00 |
| What To Eat & What Not To Eat by Dr. Swope | (60 minutes) | $20.00 |
| It's Not Too Late: Nutirtional Update by Swope/McKeever | (58 minutes) | $20.00 |
| Using Nutrition as Medicine by Swope/McKeever | (43 minutes) | $20.00 |
| You Can't Improve on God! by Lorraine Day, M.D. | (77 minutes) | $21.00 |
| Cancer Doesn't Scare Me Anymore by Lorraine Day, M.D. | (77 minutes) | $20.00 |

**INTERNATIONAL ORDERS - ALL PRICES ARE IN U.S. FUNDS**
**All Prices Subject To Change Without Prior Notice**

### SHIPPING & HANDLING

| $ AMOUNT | U.S. | CAN | INT'L | | $ AMOUNT | U.S. | CAN | INT'L |
|---|---|---|---|---|---|---|---|---|
| $ 0 and up | $ 3 | $ 6 | Call | | $ 75 and up | $ 9 | $18 | Call |
| $ 10 and up | $ 4 | $ 8 | Us | Other Case Prices By | $100 | $11 | Call | Us |
| $ 20 and up | $ 5 | $10 | Call | Request | Over $100 | | Us | |
| $ 30 and up | $ 6 | $12 | Us | | Repeat Chgs | | | |
| $ 40 and up | $ 7 | $14 | Call | | Case GLB | $15 | Call | Call |
| $ 50 and up | $ 8 | $16 | Us | | Case BYC | $15 | Us | Us |

NAME _____

ADDRESS _____

CITY / STATE / ZIP _____

PHONE  (     ) _____

| AMOUNT |
| ENCLOSED |

PLEASE CALL US WITH ANY QUESTIONS...